Yarns and Shanties

and Other Nautical Baloney

Other Books by Jim Toomey

Sherman's Lagoon: Ate That, What's Next?

Poodle: The Other White Meat

An Illustrated Guide to Shark Etiquette

Another Day in Paradise

Greetings from Sherman's Lagoon

Surf's Up!

The Shark Diaries

Catch of the Day

A Day at the Beach

Surfer Safari

Planet of the Hairless Beach Apes

Treasuries

Sherman's Lagoon 1991 to 2001:
Greatest Hits and Near Misses

In Shark Years I'm Dead: Sherman's Lagoon Turns Fifteen

Yarns and Shanties

and Other Nautical Baloney

The Twelfth Sherman's Lagoon Collection

by Jim Toomey

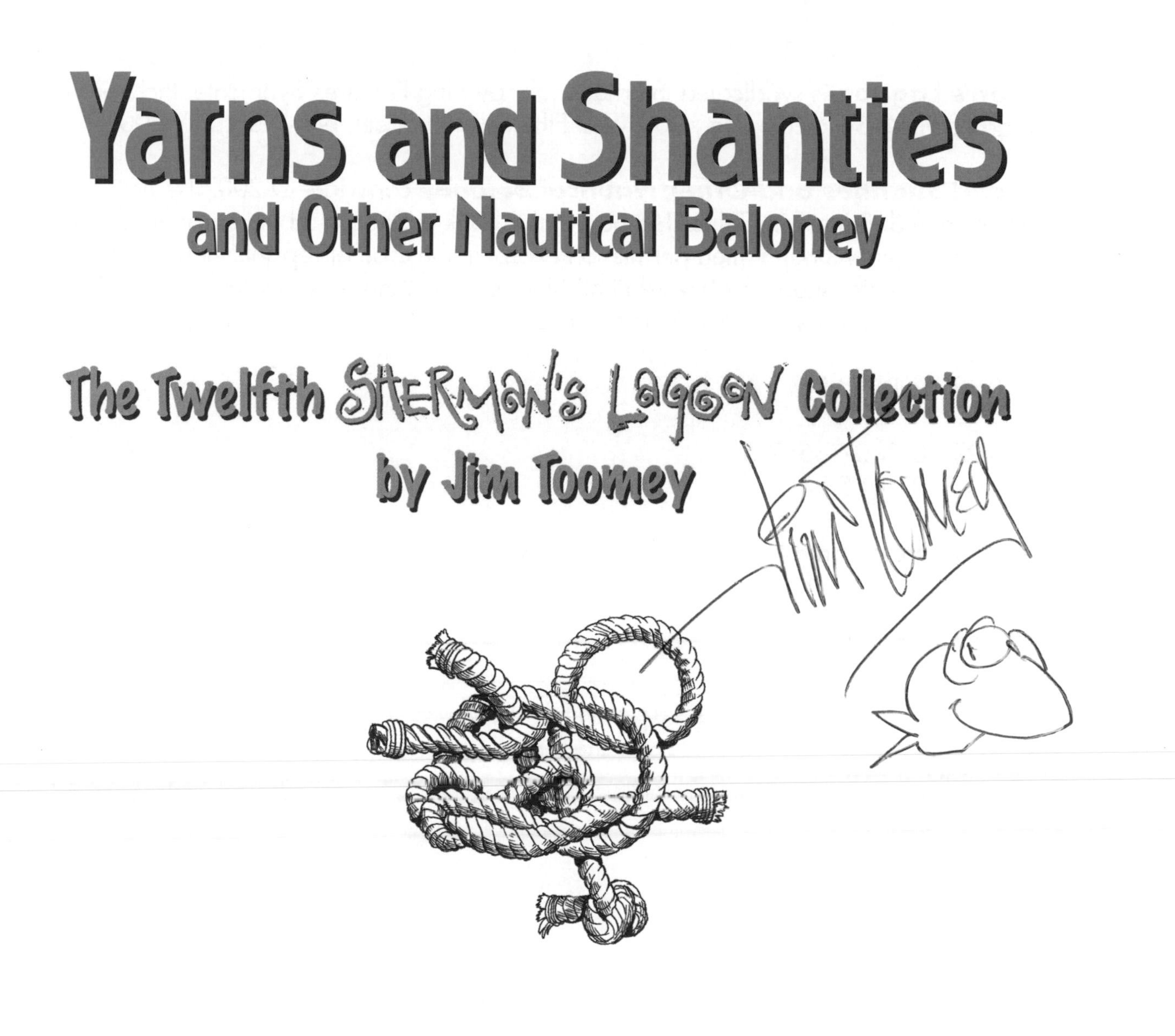

Andrews McMeel Publishing, LLC

Kansas City

Sherman's Lagoon is syndicated internationally by King Features Syndicate, Inc. For information, write King Features Syndicate, Inc., 300 West Fifty-Seventh Street, New York, NY 10019.

For information, write Andrews McMeel Publishing, LLC, an Andrews McMeel Universal company, 4520 Main Street, Kansas City, Missouri 64111.

08 09 10 11 SDB 10 9 8 7 6 5 4 3 2

ISBN-13: 978-0-7407-6557-5
ISBN-10: 0-7407-6557-4

Library of Congress Control Number: 2007925335

www.andrewsmcmeel.com

Sherman's Lagoon may be viewed on the Internet at
www.shermanslagoon.com.

To Jay Kennedy,
whose vision, imagination, and energy
helped bring so many comic strips to life,
including this one.

SO, WHY DO YOU WANT TO GO TO AUSTRALIA, ERNEST?
THE WHITSUNDAY ISLANDS, ACTUALLY.
AT A CERTAIN TIME OF YEAR, JELLYFISH ARRIVE IN LARGE NUMBERS. IT'S A SIGHT TO BEHOLD.
HMPH... INTERESTING, YET NOT ENOUGH TO CONVINCE ME TO MAKE THAT LONG JOURNEY.
THESE JELLYFISH BRING ICE CREAM TO ALL SHARKS THAT VISIT.
GO ON...
SHERMAN, SINCE WE'RE REGULAR TRAVEL COMPANIONS, I'VE TAKEN THE LIBERTY OF ASSEMBLING A LIST OF ITEMS THAT SHOULD BE IN YOUR SUITCASE.
HERE THEY ARE IN ALPHABETICAL ORDER...
DEODORANT, MOUTHWASH.
THAT'S GOOD. I ALWAYS FORGET THOSE... WHAT ELSE?
THAT'S IT. WANNA HEAR IT IN REVERSE ALPHABETICAL ORDER?
I THINK I GOT IT.

WHY ARE WE BRINGING HAWTHORNE ON THIS TRIP AGAIN?
JUST TO SHAKE THINGS UP.
BUT ALL HE DOES IS FIGHT WITH TOTAL STRANGERS.
HE NEEDS THREE A DAY TO FEEL COMPLETE.
AND LET'S BE HONEST. MOST OF THEM HAVE IT COMING.
AND ANOTHER THING, SISTER...
SHE MIGHT BE A QUOTA FILLER.

WE MUST BE GETTING CLOSE TO THE WHITSUNDAY ISLANDS. I'M SEEING AUSTRALIAN WILDLIFE.
LOOK. IT'S A KOALA.
OH MY GOSH! HE'S THE CUTEST THING EVER.
DON'T YOU JUST WANT TO GIVE HIM A BIG HUG?
YEAH, HE'S CUTE ALRIGHT.
BUT HE'S NOT CRAB CUTE.
WOW. "CRAB" AND "CUTE" IN THE SAME SENTENCE.
SHERMAN, PLEASE DON'T EMBARRASS ME IN FRONT OF OUR AUSTRALIAN FRIENDS. GOT IT?
IT'S COOL. I BRUSHED UP ON MY AUSTRALIAN. WATCH THIS.
HEY, MATE, THROW ANOTHER CHIMP ON THE BARBIE.
IT'S "SHRIMP," YOU IDIOT.
NO. I'VE GOT A DEFINITE CHIMPANZEE CRAVING.

LOOK, BOYS, THERE'S OUR FIRST JELLYFISH SIGHTING.
LATIN NAME, "CARUKIA BARNESI." THE LOCALS CALL IT "IRUKANDJI." IT'S ONE OF THE WORLD'S MOST DEADLY.
I'M NOT POSITIVE ON THE SPECIES. WE MIGHT WANT TO GET A SECOND OPINION.
I THINK IT'S A SANDWICH BAG.
LET'S GET A THIRD OPINION.

SHERMAN'S LAGOON
WHATCHA READIN', HAWTHORNE?
THE UNDERSEA ALMANAC.
THE WHAT?
IT'S A CALENDAR OF ALL THE NATURAL EVENTS OCCURRING IN THE OCEAN THIS YEAR.
I SEE THEY MOVED THE HERMIT CRAB MATING SEASON TO THE THIRD LUNAR CYCLE AFTER THE SUMMER SOLSTICE.
THAT WOULD PUT IT SOMEWHERE IN THE SECOND WEEK OF SEPTEMBER.
I DON'T KNOW WHY I WAS THINKING IT WAS GOING TO BE IN AUGUST THIS YEAR.
GOOD THING I CHECKED. MAN, I WOULD'VE BECOME THE LAUGHINGSTOCK OF THE CRAB WORLD.
DOES IT SAY ANYTHING ABOUT SHARK MATING SEASON?
LAST WEEK.

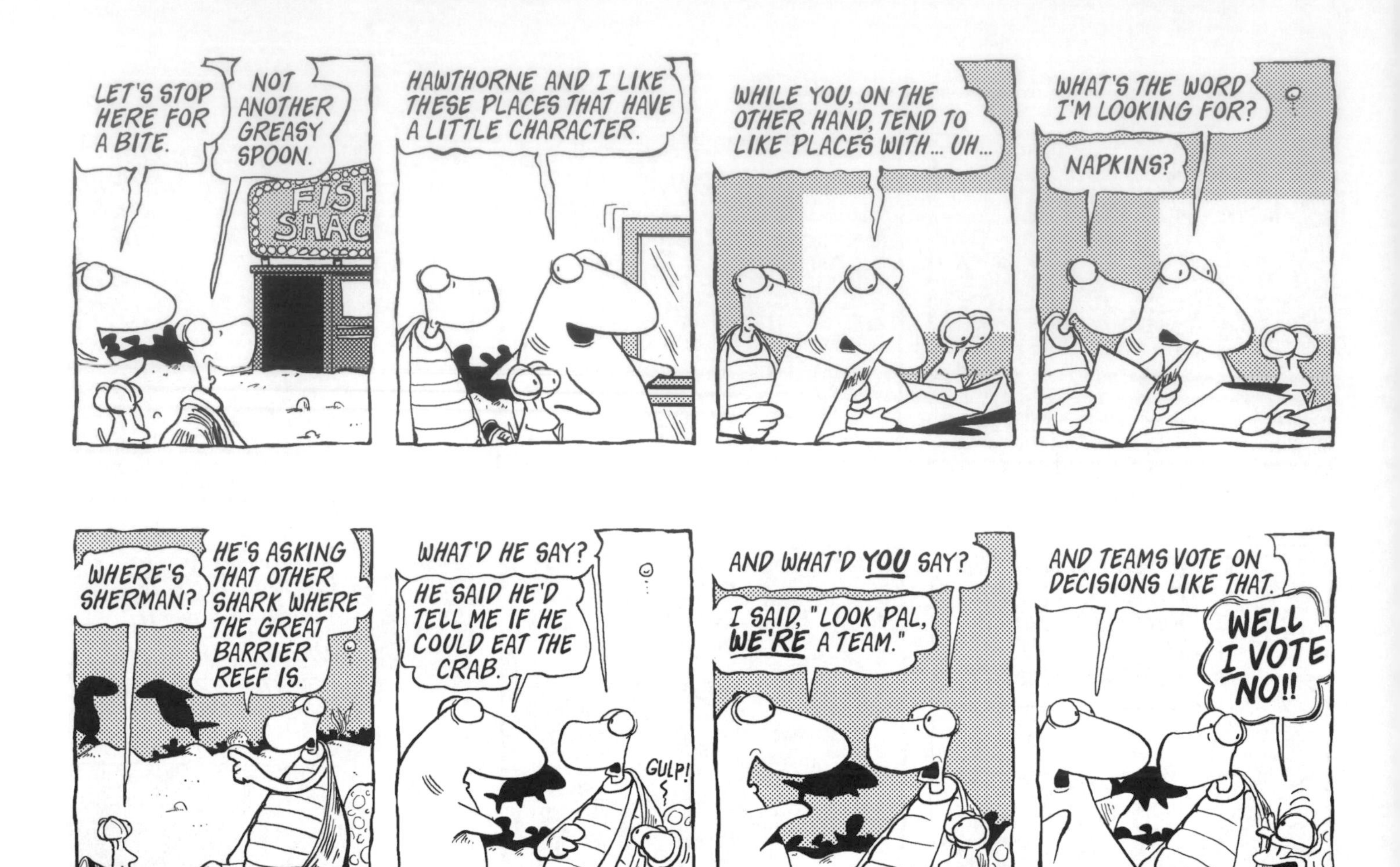
LET'S STOP HERE FOR A BITE.
NOT ANOTHER GREASY SPOON.
FISH SHAC
HAWTHORNE AND I LIKE THESE PLACES THAT HAVE A LITTLE CHARACTER.
WHILE YOU, ON THE OTHER HAND, TEND TO LIKE PLACES WITH... UH...
WHAT'S THE WORD I'M LOOKING FOR?
NAPKINS?
WHERE'S SHERMAN?
HE'S ASKING THAT OTHER SHARK WHERE THE GREAT BARRIER REEF IS.
WHAT'D HE SAY?
HE SAID HE'D TELL ME IF HE COULD EAT THE CRAB.
GULP!
AND WHAT'D YOU SAY?
I SAID, "LOOK PAL, WE'RE A TEAM."
AND TEAMS VOTE ON DECISIONS LIKE THAT.
WELL I VOTE NO!!

HAWTHORNE, COME ON! TIME'S A-WASTIN'.
HOLD YER HORSES!
I'M WRITING MY MOM A POST CARD, THANKING HER FOR LOOKING AFTER THE CRAB HOLE WHILE I'VE BEEN GONE.
I GUESS WE CAN WAIT FOR THAT.
YEAH. NOTHING MORE SPECIAL THAN MOM.
"P.S. DON'T STEAL ANYTHING."
THERE'S A HALLMARK MOMENT.

CHECK OUT THE FAKE KANGAROO POUCH I GOT AT THE WHITSUNDAY GIFT SHOP.
IT'S A PURSE.
IT'S NOT A PURSE. IT'S A POUCH.
I'M SECURE ENOUGH IN MY MASCULINITY THAT I DON'T FEEL THE NEED TO CONFORM TO SOME SOCIETAL IMAGE OF WHAT A MAN OUGHT TO BE.
WHAT'CHA GOT IN THERE?
THE NEW COSMO AND SOME EYE LINER.
WELL, THE WHITSUNDAY ISLANDS WERE GREAT, BUT I'M READY TO GET HOME.
WHITSUNDAY ISLANDS
WELCOME
WE SHOULD HIT IT. IT'S A LONG TRIP BACK.
THEY SAY THE TRIP HOME GOES A LOT FASTER.
"THEY" NEVER TRAVELLED WITH HAWTHORNE.
99 PICTURES OF ME ON THE WALL, 99 PICTURES OF ME...

I'M BACK FROM MY ROAD TRIP, MEGAN, AND IT SURE IS NICE TO BE HOME.
YEP. HOME SWEET HOME. ALMOST FORGOT WHAT IT LOOKED LIKE.
WANNA EAT OUT TONIGHT?
I'LL GET A BABYSITTER.

SHERMAN'S LAGOON

AHHHH... I LOVE WEEKENDS.

BUT YOU'RE OUT HERE IN A BEACH CHAIR SEVEN DAYS A WEEK, THORNTON.
I KNOW. BUT ON WEEKENDS I FEEL LESS GUILTY ABOUT IT.

ONCE MONDAY ROLLS AROUND AND THE REST OF THE WORLD GOES BACK TO WORK, THAT'S WHEN I GET... WELL... A LITTLE ANTSY.
ANTSY?

YEAH. THAT'S WHEN I THINK MAYBE I SHOULD GET OUT AND WORK, TOO. YOU KNOW... FIGHT THE GOOD FIGHT... MAKE THE WORLD A BETTER PLACE...

INSTEAD OF JUST SITTING ON A SUNNY BEACH IN THE TROPICS ALL DAY LONG. YOU HEAR WHAT I'M SAYING?
UH HUH.

HAWTHORNE, JUST BETWEEN YOU AND ME, I THINK I MIGHT BE EXPERIENCING THE EARLY WARNING SIGNS OF AMBITION.

HAD ME GOING FOR A MINUTE.
MORE SMOOTHIE?

HERE YA GO, BOYS. INVITATIONS TO THE GRAND OPENING OF MY GOOD OL' FASHIONED GENERAL STORE.
A GENERAL STORE?
YEP. THE KIND THAT USED TO REALLY CARE ABOUT ITS CUSTOMERS.
CHECK OUT OUR SLOGAN.
"THE SERVICE OF YESTERDAY...
...WITH THE PRICES OF TOMORROW."
WELL, I'LL BE... A GENERAL STORE.
THAT'S RIGHT, OLD TIMER.
WHEN I WAS A BOY, I USED TO WALK 13 MILES TO THE GENERAL STORE EVERY DAY JUST TO GET PENNY CANDIES. THEY WERE THE CAT'S MEOW.
WELL, TIMES HAVE CHANGED A **LITTLE** SINCE THEN.
WHAT CAN I GET FOR A PENNY?
DIRECTIONS TO ANOTHER STORE.

YOU GOT BATTERIES?
ERNEST, ERNEST, ERNEST...
THIS IS AN OLD-FASHIONED GENERAL STORE. RELAX. BROWSE. TAKE YOUR TIME. SAMPLE THE GOODS.
THIS IS A CHANCE FOR YOU YOUNG FOLKS TO GET A GLIMPSE OF WHAT LIFE USED TO BE LIKE.
I SAW BATTERIES ON YOUR WEBSITE.
AISLE THREE, BY THE X-BOXES.

WOW! HAWTHORNE, YOUR GENERAL STORE IS AWESOME!
THANKS!
ENJOY YOUR VISIT. BUY SOMETHING... OR DON'T.
WE'RE JUST AS HAPPY TO MAKE A FRIEND AS WE ARE TO MAKE A SALE.
BOY, YOU DON'T HEAR THAT MUCH THESE DAYS.
SECURITY. POSSIBLE SHOPLIFTER.
I'M ON IT, BOSS.

HOW'S THE NEW GENERAL STORE GOING?
THINGS ARE BOOMING. I'VE EVEN OPENED AN OLD-FASHIONED SODA FOUNTAIN.
SAY, YOU WANT TO BE A SODA JERK?
A **WHAT**?
"SODA JERK" IS NOT AN INSULT. IT'S A JOB TITLE... YOU'D WORK BEHIND THE COUNTER.
RIGHT NEXT TO THE SLURPEE DORK OVER THERE.
HEY, DOUG.

ERNEST, YOU'RE LATE!
WHOA, HEY...
WHAT HAPPENED TO THE LAID-BACK, KINDLY, OLD-FASHIONED GENERAL STORE ATTITUDE?
YOU'RE RIGHT, YOU'RE RIGHT. WHAT'S A FEW MINUTES WHEN WE HAVE ALL DAY. I APOLOGIZE.
CATTLE PROD HIM, SIR?
NOT UNTIL THE SECOND OFFENSE.

SHERMAN'S LAGOON
SARDINES
SO LONG, ROSCOE. WE'RE GOING TO MISS YOU...
IT WAS GOOD SWIMMING WITH YOU, ROSCOE.
ARRIVEDERCI, ROSCOE BABY. I HOPE I'M IN YOUR WILL.
ROSCOE, YOU WERE LIKE AN UNCLE TO ME.
OH, ROSCOE, WE HARDLY KNEW YE.
MAN, THESE SARDINE FUNERALS ARE ALWAYS A LITTLE CREEPY.
WHICH ONE'S ROSCOE?
THIRD FROM THE LEFT.

MY WIFE WANTS ME TO PICK UP INGREDIENTS FOR SOME EXOTIC SUSHI RECIPE OF HERS.
LET'S SEE... I NEED FERTILIZED QUAIL EGGS...
WHOA! STOP!
THIS IS A GENERAL STORE... LIKE THE GOOD OLD DAYS... WE SELL THE BASICS TO FARMERS AND TOWNFOLK. WE DON'T HAVE FERTILIZED QUAIL EGGS.
HOW 'BOUT SOME CHICKEN EGGS AND A SACK OF FERTILIZER?
BRING IT ON.

HAWTHORNE, I NEED A BAND AID THAT MATCHES MY SEA TURTLE SKIN... AND NOT LOGGERHEAD OR LEATHERBACK GREEN... MY SKIN'S MORE OLIVEY.
YOU'RE KIDDING ME!

THIS IS A GENERAL STORE. WE HAVE ONE KIND OF BAND AID AND IT'S PINK. IT APPROXIMATES THE SKIN COLOR OF THE NORTHERN-EUROPEAN HAIRLESS BEACH APE. AISLE FOUR.

THAT'S RIDICULOUS! HOW MANY OF THOSE DO YOU SELL AROUND HERE, HUH?
PLENTY, MISTER!

MY NORTHERN-EUROPEAN FRIEND CUT HIMSELF AGAIN.
AISLE FOUR.

OKAY, ERNEST, HAVE YOU ORGANIZED THIS STORE PROPERLY?
ALL ORGANIZED.

WHERE COULD I FIND UNSALTED BUTTER?
AISLE TWO. DAIRY.

WELL DONE. I MUST ADMIT, I HAD RESERVATIONS ABOUT EMPLOYING A JUVENILE DELINQUENT.
I'M LOOKING FOR BROWN SUGAR.

ITEMS THAT SOUND LIKE ROLLING STONES SONGS, AISLE SEVEN.
WE NEED TO TALK.

HAWTHORNE! YOUR GENERAL STORE! WHAT HAPPENED?
IT BURNED TO THE GROUND.
FORTUNATELY, I WAS INSURED FOR TWICE THE ACTUAL VALUE.
I KNOW WE'VE COVERED THIS BEFORE WITH YOU, BUT...
HOW EXACTLY DOES AN UNDERWATER BUSINESS BURN DOWN?
PERSISTENCE.
DID YOU SEE THAT ARTICLE ABOUT KELP IN TODAY'S PAPER?
YEAH. IT'S AMAZING STUFF.
HELPS VISION, COORDINATION, HEARING... IT EVEN GROWS BRAIN CELLS.
A SUPER FOOD EXTRAORDINAIRE.
SO HOW OFTEN DO YOU EAT IT?
NEVER. IT'S DISGUSTING.

WHADDAYA WANNA MAKE FOR DINNER? I'M STARVED.
KELP.
GROSS.
I'VE DECIDED WE NEED TO SEE IF ALL THE HYPE IS TRUE.
DON'T WORRY. WE'LL JUMP IN SLOWLY.
HOW ARE YOU PREPARING IT?
WITH THAT LITTLE BOX OVER THERE.
KELP HELPER?

Sherman's Lagoon
ZZZZZZ
LOOK AT US, MEGAN. WE'RE ACTUALLY HAVING THE PERFECT FAMILY MOMENT.
I'M SITTING HERE RELAXING, YOU'RE THERE READING A BOOK, AND HERMAN'S PLAYING WITH A NICE, EDUCATIONAL TOY.
IS THIS AN IDYLLIC IMAGE OR WHAT?
I NEVER THOUGHT WE'D HAVE A MOMENT LIKE THIS IN OUR LIVES.
WE'RE NOT.
HUH?
YOU'RE ASLEEP ON THE COUCH AS USUAL.
YOU MEAN, THIS IS ALL A DREAM?
YEP.
I USED TO HAVE MUCH BETTER DREAMS THAN THIS.
SIGN OF MIDDLE AGE.

KELP AGAIN TONIGHT?
YEP. IT'S THE NEW SUPERFOOD.
AND WE HAVE TO MAINTAIN A STEADY DIET OF IT LONG ENOUGH TO SEE THE BENEFITS.
NOT TO WORRY, I FOUND AN ENTIRE COOKBOOK OF KELP RECIPES.
WHAT'S TONIGHT'S VARIATION?
KELP ON A STICK.
CAN I JUST EAT THE STICK?
SO, IS THIS ALL-KELP DIET THAT I'VE HAD US ON DOING YOU ANY GOOD?
WHAT DO YOU MEAN BY THAT?
WELL, YOU KNOW... ARE YOU FEELING BETTER? ARE YOU REGULAR?
AM I **WHAT**?... IS THAT WHAT EIGHT YEARS OF MARRIAGE HAS DONE TO US? NOW WE CAN TALK ABOUT "REGULARITY"?
SOMETIMES A LITTLE REPRESSION CAN BE A BEAUTIFUL THING.
NOPE. OPEN MARRIAGE.

TODAY'S HEALTHY MEAL IS KELP SALAD. THIS STUFF WILL ADD YEARS TO YOUR LIFE.
TROUBLE WITH HEALTHY FOOD IS THAT IT'S SO BLAND.
I HAVE TO SMOTHER IT WITH THIS STUFF ON BEFORE I CAN EAT IT.
WHAT IS IT?
BACON FAT.
GIMME SOME OF THAT.

MEGAN, WE'VE BEEN EATING NOTHING BUT KELP FOR 10 DAYS STRAIGHT!
WHEN DO THE BENEFICIAL EFFECTS OF KELP BEGIN TO TAKE EFFECT? I'M NOT FEELING ANY DIFFERENT.
WELL, YOU'RE STARTING TO LOOK A LITTLE DIFFERENT.
I AM?
HOLD STILL.
WHAT IS IT?

SHERMAN, TURNS OUT THAT KELP ISN'T THAT NUTRITIOUS AFTER ALL. THERE'S BEEN A DECIMAL POINT ERROR.
KELP DOESN'T HAVE 500% OF THE RECOMMENDED DAILY ALLOWANCE OF VITAMINS AND MINERALS... IT'S ONLY 5%
WHAT TO DO WITH ALL OF THE WONDERFUL KELP DISHES I PREPARED... THE KELP SLAW AND THE KELP SOUP... THE KELP BURGERS AND KELP AU GRATIN... ALL THAT WORK.
TOMORROW'S TRASH DAY.
CLEARLY YOU'RE NOT AS BROKEN UP ABOUT THIS.

HOW MANY PEOPLE HAVE SIGNED THE ONLINE PETITION?
OVER 20,000.
THAT OUGHT TO GET THEIR ATTENTION.
WE'LL SUBMIT THIS TO THE GOVERNMENT AND HOPEFULLY THEY'LL HAVE THE COURAGE TO SAY "NO, NOT HERE."
ANOTHER NUCLEAR TEST?
THE WIGGLES WORLD TOUR.

SHERMAN'S LAGOON
I PICKED UP AN ESPRESSO MAKER, MEGAN. IT'S SOME FANCY ITALIAN BRAND.
LET'S HOOK THIS SUCKER UP AND MAKE ESPRESSO.
I'M PUSHING ALL THE BUTTONS. SOMETHING'S BOUND TO HAPPEN.
AH HA! A BLINKING RED LIGHT. THAT'S PROBABLY A SIGN THAT ESPRESSO IS FORTHCOMING.
WAIT A MINUTE. THIS THING PROBABLY HAS TO BE ATTACHED, WHATEVER IT IS.
WHERE ARE THE DIRECTIONS?
WHO NEEDS DIRECTIONS?
I SEE THE PROBLEM.
YOU BROUGHT HOME A PASTA MAKER.
THEN MAKE PASTA, FOR CRYING OUT LOUD!

HEY, HAWTHORNE, HOW OLD ARE YOU ANYWAYS?
ME? LATE TWENTIES.
OH. GOOD. I'M READIN' THIS ARTICLE ABOUT HERMIT CRABS AND IT SAYS THEY CAN LIVE UP TO 35 YEARS.
YOU GOT A FEW MORE YEARS LEFT IN YOU.
HE'S BEEN IN HIS LATE TWENTIES FOR A GOOD 10 YEARS NOW.
THAT WOULD EXPLAIN THE CONVULSIONS.

I HAVE AN ANNOUNCEMENT TO MAKE... I'M GIVING IT ALL UP. I'M RETIRING.
TIME HAS SLIPPED AWAY, AND I HAVE BUT A PRECIOUS FEW GOLDEN YEARS AHEAD OF ME...
SNIFF
BARELY ENOUGH TIME TO REFLECT ON ALL THE ACCOMPLISHMENTS IN MY LIFE. MY FAMILY, MY CAREER...
YOU NEVER HAD A FAMILY OR A CAREER.
I KNEW THERE WAS SOMETHING I FORGOT TO DO.

WELCOME! WELCOME TO MY RETIREMENT PARTY!
WHAT A SPREAD.
HAPPY RET
YOU REALLY WENT ALL OUT, HAWTHORNE. EVERYTHING'S SO LAVISH.
I CATERED IT MYSELF.
THE APPETIZERS ARE DAY-OLD, THE BAND IS LIP SYNCHING, AND THE "HELIUM" BALLOONS ARE FULL OF AIR.
BWA HA HA HA HA HA!
HE EVEN RIPS HIMSELF OFF.
OLD HABITS DIE HARD.

SO... RETIRING, HUH, HAWTHORNE?
YEP. I'M HANGING IT UP.
HAPPY RETIRE
WHAT ARE YOUR PLANS?
DUNNO... MAYBE YOU AND I COULD START PALLING AROUND TOGETHER.
GULP
HAPPY RETIRE
AM I DREAMING? IS THIS A NIGHTMARE?
THAT TIE'S SCARING ALL OF US.
WELL, LOOK WHO'S HERE. IT'S MR. RETIREMENT.
HEY, FILLMORE. WHAT'S UP?
HOW'S THE BOOK?
FINE.
MAYBE I'LL DO SOME READING NOW THAT I HAVE THE TIME.
GOOD IDEA. I ENCOURAGE IT.
MAYBE GET YOUR OWN BOOK.
NO, I'M GOOD. CATCH ME UP ON THE PLOT LINE HERE.
THORNTON, HOW DO YOU DO IT?
DO WHAT?
NOTHING ALL DAY! I'VE BEEN RETIRED ONLY A FEW DAYS AND I'M ALREADY GOING CRAZY!
WHICH IS WHY I'VE COME TO YOU, OH MASTER OF DOING NOTHING. WHAT IS THE ESSENCE OF NOTHINGNESS?
SILENCE.
HMPH. GOOD. I'LL HAVE TO REMEMBER THAT. "SILENCE IS THE ESSENCE OF NOTHINGNESS." WHAT ELSE?
SHUT UP.

SHERMAN'S LAGOON
I WANNA BE RICH. FILTHY RICH.
IT'S NEVER GOOD ENOUGH FOR YOU, IS IT?
HUH?
HOW WOULD BEING FILTHY RICH MAKE YOUR LIFE BETTER?
YOU'D HAVE MORE STUFF, BUT WOULD YOU BE HAPPIER?
IF YOU'RE NOT HAPPY NOW, BEING RICH ISN'T GOING TO DO IT.
IMAGINE THAT YOU'RE RICH. YOU'RE SITTING IN YOUR MANSION HAVING A MARTINI. BUT IT'S THE SAME OLD YOU...
AND NOW YOU'RE NOT HAPPY BECAUSE YOUR MARTINI ISN'T DRY ENOUGH, AND YOU DON'T LIKE WHAT THE DECORATORS DID WITH THE MANSION.
YOU FOLLOW ME? THE BAR KEEPS GETTING RAISED.
I JUST NOW NOTICED YOU DON'T HAVE ANY EARS.
OKAY. THAT WAS A WASTE OF BREATH.

SHERMAN, LET'S GO GOLFING!
HAWTHORNE, I'M NOT RETIRED LIKE YOU.
I CAN'T JUST GO GOLFING AT THE DROP OF A HAT.
I'VE GOT SOME STUFF TO FINISH UP. THEN MAYBE WE CAN THINK ABOUT GOING GOLFING.
WHERE WERE WE, ERNEST?
I SCRATCHED. YOUR SHOT.
BOY, RETIREMENT IS BORING.
GET A HOBBY.
LIKE STAMP COLLECTING OR BIRD WATCHING... TRY DRAWING A COMIC STRIP IF YOU CAN'T DO ANYTHING ELSE.
I'VE GOT A GREAT HOBBY ALREADY. HANGING OUT WITH YOU GUYS.
YOU NEED ONE THAT WON'T GET YOU KILLED.
NOT FOLLOWING.

HAWTHORNE'S RETIREMENT IS DRIVING ME NUTS. HE BUGS ME NONSTOP.
HE HANGS OUT WITH ME AND ASKS DUMB COMPUTER QUESTIONS.
HE ACCUSED ME OF HAVING BAD BREATH.
UMMM, HOW IS THE BREATH COMMENT RETIREMENT RELATED?
HE SAID IT WHILE WHITTLING.

WE NEED TO FIND SOMETHING THAT WILL KEEP HAWTHORNE BUSY IN RETIREMENT.
ANY SUGGESTIONS?
HOW ABOUT A BAGPIPE?
OOH! OR A BIG BOOK OF KNOCK KNOCK JOKES!
HOW ABOUT SHERMAN GETS KICKED OFF THE SUGGESTION COMMITEE?
SECOND.

HAWTHORNE, WE'VE COME UP WITH A GREAT WAY FOR YOU TO SPEND RETIREMENT.
TA-DAH! AN INFORMATION BOOTH! YOU'LL SPEND YOUR TIME HERE, ANSWERING IMPORTANT QUESTIONS.
INFO
INF
IS THIS JUST A WAY FOR YOU GUYS TO GET RID OF ME?
ANSWER QUESTIONS, SILLY. DON'T ASK THEM.
INF

EXCUSE ME. WHICH WAY TO DOLPHIN COVE?
QUARTER MILE THAT WAY. HANG A LEFT AT THE SHIPWRECK.
INFORMATION
THANKS. WHAT DO I OWE YOU?
NOTHING. INFORMATION IS FREE.
NOT THESE DAYS. THIS IS THE INFORMATION AGE. INFORMATION IS MONEY.
KA-CHING!
DID YOUR BODY JUST MAKE A CASH REGISTER NOISE?
THAT ANSWER'S GONNA COST YOU.

SHERMAN'S LAGOON
WANNA BORROW SOME STUFF?
WHAT KIND OF STUFF?
WHY ARE YOU LENDING OUT YOUR STUFF?
I NEED TO CREATE ROOM FOR NEW STUFF.
THEN SELL SOME OF YOUR OLD STUFF.
NO!!

ALL KINDS OF STUFF. FURNITURE, KNICK-KNACKS, CURIOS, MILITARY DECORATIONS. I HAVE A NICE CUCKOO CLOCK.

WELL, THEN, YOU'RE JUST GOING TO HAVE TO STOP BUYING NEW STUFF.
I'M TOO YOUNG TO QUIT BUYING STUFF. THERE'S ALL KINDS OF STUFF OUT THERE I STILL NEED TO OWN!

HERE. TAKE THIS CUCKOO CLOCK. JUST GIVE IT A GOOD HOME.
NO! I DON'T WANT YOUR STUFF! GO AWAY!

HOW MUCH FOR THE ROCKING CHAIR?
BEAT IT!

SO I HEAR YOU'VE TURNED THIS FRIENDLY NEIGHBORHOOD INFORMATION BOOTH INTO A FOR-PROFIT ENTERPRISE.
YES.
AND THAT'LL BE FIVE DOLLARS.
WHAT'LL BE FIVE DOLLARS?
THE ANSWER TO YOUR QUESTION ABOUT MY BUSINESS.
MAN, IS THIS A SCAM OR WHAT?
WANT THE ANSWER? THREE DOLLARS.

I HEAR YOU'RE RUNNING AN OVER-THE-COUNTER SEARCH ENGINE. I NEED INFO. FAST.
HIT ME.
Crabble
WHERE ARE ALL THE GOOD SALES AT TODAY?
ONE MOMENT WHILE I CONSULT MY DATABASE.
HMMM...
I COULD'VE JUST LOOKED IN THE PAPER!
HOW ARE YOU FOR RADIAL TIRES?
Crabble

SO, WHY SHOULD I USE THE CRABBLE SEARCH ENGINE INSTEAD OF GOOGLE?
GOOD QUESTION.
Crabble
BECAUSE WITH CRABBLE YOU GET PERSONAL INTERACTION. GOOGLE'S JUST A COLD, FACELESS WEBSITE.
YEAH, BUT GOOGLE NEVER HAS SPINACH IN ITS TEETH.
THAT'S JALAPENO.
Crabble

I'VE GOT A RATHER PERSONAL QUESTION FOR CRABBLE.
SPEAK TO THE ALL-KNOWING ONE, OH DESPERATE TURTLE.
Crabble
THERE'S BIG BUCKS IN IT IF YOU CAN HELP ME.
MUSIC TO MY EARS. WHAT'S YOUR QUESTION?
Crabble
WHAT'S THE MOST EFFECTIVE WAY TO WOO A SHE-TURTLE.
HMMM...
SEARCHING THE DATABASE?
LOOKING UP "WOO."
HAWTHORNE, YOU CLOSED YOUR INFORMATION BOOTH. WHY?
MY HEART JUST WASN'T IN IT.
CLOSED
WHAT IS YOUR HEART INTO, THEN?
MAKING GOBS OF MONEY, PREFERABLY BY TAKING ADVANTAGE OF OTHERS.
Crabble
DO THE REST OF YOUR ORGANS FEEL THAT WAY?
'FRAID SO.
LOOK AT THAT POOR DOG.
TIED DOWN. TETHERED. HIS SPIRIT BROKEN. NO CONTROL OVER HIS DESTINY.
SHERMAN! GET HOME IMMEDIATELY!
I WAS JUST HEADING THAT WAY, DEAR.
THINK HE SEES THE IRONY?
NOT WITHOUT PERMISSION.

SHERMAN'S LAGOON
BOY, I'M GLAD THAT FISHING TOURNAMENT IS OVER.
ROGER THAT.
WHO'S ROGER, ANYWAY?
GOT ME. IT'S PILOT LINGO.
I GUESS ROGER WAS SOME CONTROL TOWER DUDE WHO UNDERSTOOD EVERYTHING THE FIRST TIME YOU SAID IT TO HIM.
YOU KNOW, SHERMAN, IT OCCURS TO ME... THE WORLD COULD USE A WORD THAT MEANS THE OPPOSITE OF "ROGER."
SOMETHING THAT SAYS "WHOA, TALK SLOWER. YOU'RE CONFUSING ME. I DON'T HAVE THE BRAIN POWER TO PROCESS WHAT YOU'RE SAYING AT THE RATE YOU'RE SAYING IT."
I'VE GOT IT! FROM NOW ON, I'LL SAY "SHERMAN"!
RUN THAT BY ME AGAIN.
ROGER.

WHACK!
BING!
WHACK!
SO, IS THAT A BIRDIE?
I'D SAY THAT'S A LAWSUIT.
OH MY, WHAT A STORY.
HIT ME.
OFF THE COAST OF JAPAN, GIANT JELLYFISH HAVE TAKEN OVER.
GROSS.
THESE THINGS ARE LIKE SIX FEET ACROSS. CHECK OUT THE PHOTO.
HOLY SCHMOKES. YOU'D BE IN HEAVEN.
DON'T YOU EAT JELLYFISH?
NOT IN BULK.

HELLO THERE. I'M NEW AROUND HERE.
AUUGH!!
I HEARD ABOUT YOU! DON'T EAT ME! I'M TOO PRETTY TO DIE!
THE GIANT JELLYFISH ARE HERE!
AND LOOK RIGHT HERE! HE ZAPPED ME WITH HIS LASER VISION!
THAT LOOKS LIKE A CROCK POT BURN.

HELLO THERE. PLEASE DON'T FREAK OUT.
YOU'RE ONE OF THOSE GIANT JELLYFISH EVERYONE'S TALKING ABOUT.
YEP.
ARE YOU HERE TO WREAK HAVOC ON OUR LAGOON?
HEAVENS NO.
ARE YOU HERE TO TAKE MY BLENDER?
NO.
THEN WE'RE COOL.
WHERE'S THAT GIANT FREAK JELLYFISH?
LAST I SAW, HE WAS HEADING TOWARDS THORNTON.
OH, NO...
POOR OLD LAZY, SLOW, SMOOTHIE-DRINKING THORNTON DOESN'T STAND A CHANCE.
AAAUUUGH!
BRAIN FREEZE. ROOKIE MISTAKE.

THE MONSTER JELLYFISH HAS GOT ERNEST!
NO!!
NOT MY LITTLE BUDDY ERNEST! HE'S TOO YOUNG!
HEY, JELLYFISH! TAKE HIM, NOT ME!
DON'T YOU MEAN "TAKE ME, NOT HIM"?
I WAS POINTING AT YOU.

SHERMAN'S LAGOON
ARE YOU JUST GOING TO SIT THERE ALL DAY?
MEGAN, I THOUGHT TODAY WAS MY "SPACE" DAY.
OH, RIGHT. A MAN NEEDS HIS SPACE.
THAT'S WHAT WE AGREED ON.
HOW MUCH SPACE IS THE MAN OF THE HOUSE IN NEED OF?
THE IMMEDIATE VICINITY WOULD BE NICE.
SURE THAT'S ENOUGH?
I'LL TAKE AN EXPANDED BUFFER ZONE, AS LONG AS YOU'RE OFFERING.
FINE. I'LL GO SHOPPING.
ALL THIS SPACE IS NOW OFFICIALLY YOURS.
THESE LITTLE VICTORIES DON'T COME VERY OFTEN. THEY NEED TO BE SAVORED.
HIGH FIVE.
HERE. VACUUM YOUR SPACE.
BACK AT YA.

ERNEST! WE'LL SAVE YOU FROM THAT EVIL GIANT JELLYFISH!
NOOOO! WE'RE TOO LATE!! HE'S ALREADY...
...READING HIM HIS FAVORITE STORY.
"COMPUTER HACKING FOR FUN AND PROFIT... CHAPTER ONE..."

MEGAN, TURNS OUT THIS MONSTER JELLYFISH THAT INVADED OUR LAGOON IS ACTUALLY NOT A BAD GUY AFTERALL.
OH YEAH?
YEAH. I THINK WE SHOULD LET HIM STAY.
I THINK THAT'S A BAD IDEA.
I THINK YOU'D LIKE HIM ONCE YOU GOT TO KNOW HIM.
I ALREADY DON'T LIKE HIM.
HE'S JUST AN ENORMOUS SLIMY BLOB WITH NO CENTRAL NERVOUS SYSTEM.
WHAT'S NOT TO LIKE?

IS THAT SHERMAN I SEE OVER THERE WITH THAT MONSTER JELLYFISH?
YEP.
THEY SEEM TO BE HITTING IT OFF.
UH-HUH.
WHAT DO A LAZY, STUPID SHARK AND A GIANT JELLYFISH HAVE IN COMMON?
A LOT, APPARENTLY.
THIS IS THE SWEET SPOT. ONE GOOD SLAP HERE AND I CAN JIGGLE FOR TEN MINUTES.
CAN'T TOUCH THAT.

GOOD HEAVENS! WHAT HAPPENED TO YOU?
GOT CLIPPED BY AN OUTBOARD MOTOR.
THAT MUST'VE HURT.
NAH. A JELLYFISH DOESN'T FEEL MUCH PAIN.
I KINDA LIKE THE NEW LOOK.
THEY COULD'VE TAKEN A LITTLE MORE OFF THE SIDES.
I'VE PAID TEN BUCKS AND GOTTEN WORSE.
WHOA NELLY! WHAT HAPPENED TO YOU?
I DRIFTED INTO SOME RAZOR-SHARP CORAL.
THAT MUST'VE HURT.
NAH. JELLYFISH FEEL NO PAIN. WE MAY BE SPINELESS, BUT WE'RE NOT WIMPS.
BOY, I WISH I COULD BE SO NONCHALANT ABOUT THESE THINGS.
YOU DROPPED A PIECE OF SOMETHING.
NOT VITAL. KEEP IT. MAKES GOOD SUSHI.

WHAT'S WITH THE SUITCASE? YOU TAKING OFF?
YEP. I'M GONNA DRIFT ON OUTTA HERE.
I'M NOT REALLY INTO THE... UH... ALTERNATIVE CULTURE AROUND HERE.
IF YOU STICK AROUND, I'M SURE YOU'LL FIND WE...
ARM PIT NOISE-ATHON STARTS TOMORROW! HEY! BET YOU'RE A NATURAL!
FWAP! FWAP!
I, UH, REALLY MUST BE GOING.
TAKE ME WITH YOU?

SHERMAN'S LAGOON
HEY, SHERMAN, WANNA HIT THE LINKS THIS AFTERNOON?
CAN'T. CABLE GUY'S COMING.
SO, YOU HAVE TO SIT HERE AND KILL TIME UNTIL HE SHOWS UP?
THAT'S THE DEAL.
WHEN'S HE SUPPOSED TO COME?
SAYS HERE SOMETIME BETWEEN 8 AND 6.
THEY DID THAT TO ME.
"TODAY, TOMORROW, OR POSSIBLY THE NEXT DAY."
YEP.
"MAYBE THIS WEEK OR MAYBE THE NEXT. IT'S BEYOND OUR CONTROL."
"DURING THE MONTH OF APRIL, OR ANOTHER MONTH WITH AN 'R' IN IT."
SOUNDS FAMILIAR.
"YOU NEVER KNOW WHEN WE'LL KNOCK ON YOUR DOOR. JUST BE THERE WHEN WE DO."
"WE DON'T LIKE TO BE KEPT WAITING."
THAT'S THE PART THAT BURNS ME UP.

UH, OH. I KNOW THAT HAT.
YESSIRREE. IT'S THAT TIME OF YEAR WHEN GREEN SEA TURTLES MIGRATE TO ASCENSION ISLAND.
I'M OFF TO TRY TO WIN THE HEART OF SOME LOVELY SHE-TURTLE.
ANY ADVICE YOU LIKE TO SHARE ON THE SUBJECT OF ROMANCE?
OH, YOU KNOW, SAME THING I ALWAYS SAY...
JUST **DON'T** BE YOURSELF.
GEE, THANKS.

OFF TO ASCENSION ISLAND?
YEP. THIS IS MY YEAR.
IT'S GOTTA HAPPEN SOMETIME. 'CUZ, I FIGURE, IF SOMEBODY LIKE **SHERMAN** CAN GET A GIRL...
HEY! MY HUSBAND HAPPENS TO BE QUITE A CATCH, BUSTER!
SWEETIE, I'M BEGINNING TO SUSPECT THIS "PREPARATION H" STUFF DOESN'T MAKE TEETH ANY WHITER.
BAD TIMING, DEAR.

I'M OFF TO ASCENSION ISLAND TO TRY TO FIND A SEA TURTLE MATE.
AND YOU'RE LOOKING FOR ADVICE ON ROMANCE FROM THE MAN.
UH, NO. NOT REALLY.
YOU KNOW WHAT MAKES WOMEN HAPPY?
WHAT?
NOTHING! AT LEAST THE ONES I'VE DATED. THEY'RE NEVER HAPPY!
SO, MAYBE THERE'S A DIRECT RELATIONSHIP BETWEEN NOT HAPPY AND DATING YOU.
BEWARE! THEY CRAVE SINCERITY.

I'LL LEAVE YOU WITH ONE GOLDEN RULE ABOUT WOMEN THAT I REPEAT TO MYSELF EVERY NIGHT BEFORE I GO TO SLEEP. IT'S NOT DEEP, BUT IT IS WORTH REMEMBERING...

WOMEN ARE LIKE SMOOTHIES...

OR MAYBE IT'S WOMEN ARE **NOT** LIKE SMOOTHIES...
CAN THIS WAIT?

WELCOME TO THE PANAMA CANAL. FOR WHAT PURPOSE ARE YOU PASSING THROUGH?
OUT OF MY WAY. I'M SAVING THE PLANET.
YOU SEE, I'M A RARE SEA TURTLE, AND I MUST GET TO THE ATLANTIC OCEAN TO BREED.
BY BREEDING, I'LL ALSO BE PRESERVING BIODIVERSITY, THUS SAVING THE PLANET. SO LET ME THROUGH.
I'M NOT SO SURE WE SHOULD BE LETTING THE LIKES OF YOU BREED. LET ME CHECK WITH THE MANAGER.
I'LL BREED ANYWAY! YOU CAN'T STOP ME!

WHAT'S GOING ON? WHY ISN'T EVERYONE ON THE ISLAND?
IT'S BEEN INVADED BY HUMANS.
APPARENTLY THEIR PLANE CRASHED AND THEY'RE STRANDED.
STRANDED? MAYBE THEY'RE...
"LOST." KNOW WHAT I MEAN, LADIES? HUH?
WINK WINK
YOU DON'T WATCH MUCH TV, DO YOU?
HE'S THE WEIRD ONE I WAS TELLING YOU ABOUT.

SHERMAN'S LAGOON
I THINK I'M GOING TO CRY.
WHAT'S WRONG, MEGAN?
NOTHING. I JUST FEEL LIKE A GOOD CRY.
YOU DON'T JUST CRY FOR NO REASON. ARE YOU SAD?
MAYBE. OR MAYBE IT'S A HAPPY CRY.
YOU DON'T KNOW?
IT'S NOT SOMETHING YOU CAN ANALYZE. IT'S A GIRL THING.
I'LL BET I CAN FIGURE IT OUT.
LET'S SEE... SOMETHING IS MAKING YOU HAPPY OR SAD...
SOME THING OR SOME NON-THING.
RIGHT. IT'S EITHER A THING OR A NON-THING... THAT'S A START. IS IT REAL OR IMAGINARY?
BOTH.
I KNEW IT. WE'RE ZEROING IN ON THE PROBLEM. SO, THIS REAL OR IMAGINARY, HAPPY-SAD, THING OR NON-THING, IS IT... UH...
... IS IT SORT OF LIKE BEING HUNGRY?
GO PLAY GOLF.

ON YOUR WAY TO ASCENSION ISLAND?
YEAH.
MAYBE WE COULD HAVE DINNER THERE.
DON'T TAKE THIS PERSONALLY, BUT NOT IF YOU WERE THE LAST TURTLE ON EARTH.
WHAT OTHER WAY COULD I POSSIBLY TAKE IT?
MAYBE WITH A BREATH MINT!

MAYBE WE CAN SCARE THESE LOST HUMANS OFF ASCENSION ISLAND.
HOW?
WELL, WHAT'S THE ONE THING THAT HUMANS FEAR THE MOST?
GHOSTS?
NO.
SNAKES?
NOPE.
CARBS?
BINGO! WE NEED A POTATO LAUNCHER.

SO, HOW CAN WE SCARE THESE LOST HUMANS OFF OUR ISLAND?
WELL...
RUMOR HAS IT THERE'S A TUNNEL THAT LEADS TO A HATCH IN THE MIDDLE OF THE ISLAND.
IF ONE OF US COULD HIDE IN IT, THEY COULD REALLY SCARE 'EM WHEN THEY OPEN IT.
I'LL DO IT.
WELL, HOW'D IT GO?
NOT GOOD. I PACKED FOR FUN, NOT SCARY.

SO THERE I WAS SCRATCHING MY...
HOLD THAT THOUGHT. I'M GETTING A TEXT MESSAGE.
WHAT IS IT?
IT'S FROM FILLMORE. HE SAYS HUMANS HAVE INVADED ASCENSION ISLAND.
HE SAYS, "THEY'VE MESSED UP THE SEA TURTLE MATING GROUNDS. THINGS DON'T LOOK GOOD FOR ME THIS MATING SEASON."
AS OPPOSED TO HIS OTHER MATING SEASONS?
"TELL SHERMAN TO SHUT UP."
WE HAVE ONLY ONE DAY LEFT IN THE SEA TURTLE MATING SEASON!
WE NEED THESE HUMANS OFF OUR ISLAND NOW! LET'S RECLAIM WHAT'S OURS!
CHARGE!!
ARE THOSE SEA TURTLES COMING THIS WAY?
THEY HAVE BEEN FOR AN HOUR NOW.

WELL, THOSE "LOST" PEOPLE FINALLY GOT THE HECK OFF OUR ISLAND.
WHAT A RELIEF.
BUT NOW WE'VE ONLY GOT A COUPLE HOURS LEFT IN THE MATING SEASON.
SO, SINCE YOU'RE HERE AND I'M HERE, AND, WELL... YOU KNOW... I WAS WONDERING...
IF I FELT AS DESPERATE AS YOU LOOK?
IN SO MANY WORDS.

SHERMAN'S LAGOON
ARE YOU SURE THIS RECIPE IS GOING TO WORK?
SURE I'M SURE. THIS ROCK IS MAGIC. JUST THROW IT IN A POT OF WATER AND YOU'LL GET SOUP.
OKAY.
PLOP!
IT'S NOT DOING MUCH.
IT NEEDS SOMETHING. MAYBE A CARROT.
ONE CARROT.
STILL MISSING SOMETHING. A COUPLE OF ONIONS WOULD DO THE TRICK.
RIGHT.
HAVE YOU GOT A BOUILLON CUBE?
COMING UP.
WHAT THE HECK. THROW IN A POTATO. COULDN'T HURT.
LOVE THE SOUP.
WASN'T MUCH TILL I ADDED THE LOBSTER.

HOW'S MY DAY LOOK?
PRETTY LIGHT... JUST A BEACH SCARE AT NOON.
SQUIDOS
YOU'VE PROBABLY GOT TIME TO HIT THE GYM IF YOU WANT.
SQUIDOS
SQUIDOS
HA! HA! HA!
THE GYM! THAT'S PRICELESS!
SQUIDOS
HEY, FILLMORE, NICE GARDEN.
I GOT AN EARLY START THIS YEAR.
GARDENING IS THE ONE THING THAT KEEPS ME CENTERED.
WITH ALL THE VIOLENCE AND CONFUSION IN THE WORLD, I NEED SOMETHING CALM AND PEACEFUL.
SEA CUCUMBERS ARE GETTING AWAY.
HAND ME THE TASER.

WHATCHA DOIN', ERNEST?
CREATING A SPREADSHEET.
WHAT'S A SPREADSHEET?
SEE ALL THOSE LITTLE SQUARES? YOU CAN WRITE STUFF IN EACH ONE.
COOL.
THIS ONE CONTAINS ALL MY PERSONAL INFORMATION.

YOU'RE A MEMBER OF THE WHITE HOUSE PRESS CORPS?
I MOSTLY HECKLE.

SO, HOW DOES A SPREADSHEET WORK?
WELL, FIRST...
TAP TAP TAP TAP TAP TAP TAP
...I FEED LOTS OF INFORMATION INTO THE COMPUTER.
TAP TAP TAP TAP TAP TAP
HOW DO YOU KNOW WHEN YOU'VE GOT ENOUGH IN THERE?
TAP TAP TAP TAP TAP TAP
BURP!
THAT SHOULD DO IT.

SO, ONCE YOU ENTER ALL THIS INFORMATION INTO YOUR SPREADSHEET, WHAT HAPPENS NEXT?

WELL, IT'S A TOOL FOR ORGANIZING YOUR DATA. IT'LL PARSE AND SORT AND CALCULATE. YOU CAN USE IT TO LOOK FOR TRENDS AND REOCCURENCES.

SO, BASICALLY, IT'S LIKE A WAFFLE IRON.
WAS THERE A WARRANTY ON THAT BRAIN?

SO, I WANT TO SEE THIS SPREADSHEET YOU'RE WORKING ON. WHAT'S SO SPECIAL ABOUT IT?
I'VE ENTERED MY WHOLE LIFE INTO IT. EVERYTHING I DO, EVERYONE I KNOW, MY HOPES, MY DREAMS.
AND, YOU KNOW WHAT? ON A SPREADSHEET, MY LIFE BEGINS TO MAKE SENSE. IT'S ALL THERE.
IT'S JUST A MACHINE, ERNEST. WHEN YOU'RE READY FOR REAL INTERACTION, LET ME KNOW.
don't listen to him, ernest. he's just jealous.
WHOA.

SHERMAN'S LAG
NOW THERE'S A BEAUTY. WEST INDIAN FIGHTING CONCH.
LET'S SEE IF IT FITS.
A HERMIT CRAB CHANGES HIS SHELL BUT A FEW TIMES IN HIS LONG LIFE, AND YOU'RE ABOUT TO WITNESS IT.
JUST MY LUCK, I GUESS.
THIS IS A VERY DELICATE OPERATION.
I'M SURE IT IS.
THE HERMIT CRAB IS MOST VULNERABLE TO PREDATORS WHEN HE'S BETWEEN SHELLS.
FASCINATING.
BET YOU DIDN'T REALIZE THAT CHANGING SHELLS COULD BE SO DANGEROUS.
I DO NOW.
YOU'RE PROBABLY WONDERING HOW A CRAB MY AGE STAYS SO FIT.
NOPE. JUST GET ON WITH IT.

I HEAR THIS SPREADSHEET OF YOURS CAN PREDICT STUFF.
SURE CAN.
FINE. THEN WHO WILL WIN THE NEXT AMERICAN IDOL?
TAP TAP TAP TAP TAP TAP
HMPH. JUST AS I THOUGHT. NOTHING.
WHY DIDN'T YOU TELL HIM?
because who gives a rat's tail?
OH WISE SPREADSHEET, WHAT ADVICE DO YOU HAVE FOR ME TODAY?
avoid the crab at all costs.
YO, ERNEST!
STAY RIGHT THERE! NOT A STEP CLOSER!
HUH?
WHAM!
NOT COOL, ERNEST!
ANYTHING ELSE?

ERNEST, CAN I ASK YOUR CLAIRVOYANT SPREADSHEET A LITTLE QUESTION?
YOU MAY.
WILL KELLY EVER GO OUT WITH ME?
no.
no no no. not in your wildest dreams. not if you were the last turtle on earth. no no no.
ONE "NO" WAS PLENTY. THANK YOU.

ERNEST! I'VE GOT AN IMPORTANT PERSONAL QUESTION FOR YOUR MAGIC SPREADSHEET!
WELL, ALL RIGHT...
WILL THE PISTONS COVER THE SPREAD IN TONIGHT'S GAME?
RATTLE RATTLE
WHAT ARE YOU DOING? IT'S NOT A MAGIC EIGHT BALL!
WHAT KIND OF ANSWER IS "CATASTROPHIC SYSTEM FAILURE"?
I HEARD HAWTHORNE MADE YOUR COMPUTER CRASH.
YEP. LOST EVERYTHING, INCLUDING MY MAGIC SPREADSHEET.
TAP TAP
ALL THAT HARD WORK UP IN SMOKE.
YEP.
YET ANOTHER REASON TO AVOID HARD WORK.
YOUR LIST IS LONG.

READING ANOTHER BOOK, HUH, FILLMORE?
YEP.

WHY READ A BOOK ABOUT SOMETHING WHEN YOU CAN GO OUT AND EXPERIENCE THE REAL THING?

AUGH!

I READ A BOOK ABOUT SEA URCHINS.
SO WHY DIDN'T YOU WARN ME?

SHERMAN'S

HOW'S THE FISHING TOURNAMENT GOING?

THAT'S NINE FISH THEY'VE CAUGHT SO FAR.
IT'S NOT LOOKING GOOD.

NINE TO ONE.
WE'RE COMING BACK.

NEW VIDEO CAMERA?
YEP.
NOW THAT I'M A FATHER, I NEED TO CAPTURE LIFE'S PRECIOUS MOMENTS.
WHAT HAVE YOU CAPTURED SO FAR?
A ONE-HANDED DIAPER CHANGE GONE HORRIBLY WRONG.
SO, YOU WANNA START A PODCAST, HUH?
ONCE YOU HELP ME WITH ALL THE TECHNICAL MUMBO JUMBO.
PLUG THIS IN HERE...
UH, HUH.
... AND THAT'S IT.
YOU WANNA SEE IT AGAIN?
WITHOUT ALL THAT FANCY WRIST WORK.
WHATCHA WATCHING?
SHERMAN'S VERY FIRST LIVE PODCAST.
IT'S JUST A SHOT OF HIS EMPTY LIVING ROOM. WHERE IS HE?
FLUSH!
HI, I'M SHERMAN. WELCOME TO MY FIRST...
SHERMAN!
GO WASH YOUR FINS!
I'M PODCASTING, MEGAN!

IN TODAY'S PODCAST I'M GOING TO SHARE ONE OF MY FAVORITE SHARK RECIPES.
START WITH A THREE-WEEK-OLD SUN-DRIED FLOUNDER...
ADD A SPLASH OF PICKLE JUICE...
DISGUSTING, BUT I'M STILL CURIOUS.
... PUREE THREE LARGE SEA SLUGS...
SLOW DOWN!

IN TODAY'S PODCAST, I THOUGHT WE'D CHECK OUT THE FUNNIES.
HEH HEH...
SHOULDN'T HE READ THEM OUT LOUD?
TOO OBVIOUS.

YOU GUYS BEEN WATCHING MY PODCASTS?
YEAH. GOOD STUFF.
I BEG TO DIFFER. THEY'RE PAINFULLY BORING. TWO THUMBS WAY DOWN.
YOU NEED TO SPICE 'EM UP A LITTLE. YOU KNOW... LET US IN ON A FEW SECRETS.
TODAY WITH OUR HIDDEN CAMERA WE RECORDED FILLMORE'S STRANGE LITTLE MORNING WORKOUT.
ABOUT YOURSELF!

SHERMAN'S LAGOON
HEY, CRABCAKE, WHERE ARE YOU OFF TO IN SUCH A HURRY?
JUST HEADING THIS WAY.
WHY IS IT ANIMALS ARE ALWAYS GOING SOMEWHERE?
GOT ME.
THE BIRDS ARE ALWAYS FLYING SOMEWHERE... THE FISH ARE ALWAYS SWIMMING SOMEWHERE...
EVEN THE BUGS HAVE SOME PLACE TO BE.
WHERE ARE THEY ALL GOING? DO THEY HAVE MEETINGS? IS THERE A PARTY THAT I DON'T KNOW ABOUT?
THEY'RE JUST SCURRYING AROUND.
THEY SCURRY, HUH?
BIRDS DO IT. BEES DO IT. EVEN POLAR BEARS DO IT. NORMAL ONES, ANYWAY.
GO AHEAD... TRY IT. SCURRY SOMEWHERE. YOU'LL FEEL BETTER FOR IT.
OH, WHAT THE HECK.
I CAN DO THIS.
LOOKS LIKE WE MAY HAVE TO SURGICALLY REMOVE THE BEACH CHAIR.

AS YOU MIGHT IMAGINE, IT'S HARD WORK FINDING QUALITY MATERIAL FOR A DAILY PODCAST.
AND RATHER THAN RESORT TO CHEAP SHOTS, I'VE DECIDED TO TAKE THE HIGH ROAD.
SHOOT.
OH, WHAT THE HECK... MEGAN SNORES LIKE A LONGSHOREMAN.
THAT'S MY BOY!
HI, I'M MEGAN, FILLING IN FOR SHERMAN ON HIS DAILY PODCAST.
UMPH!
IT'S COME TO MY ATTENTION THAT SHERMAN'S BEEN SPREADING HORRIBLE RUMORS ABOUT ME.
GETTING GOOD.
SO, THIS WILL BE HIS LAST PODCAST... SHERMAN, WOULD YOU LIKE TO SAY "BYE" TO YOUR VIEWERS?
UMPH
AAUUGH!
CLOSE ENOUGH.

ERNEST, **YOU'RE** PAINTING?
I HEARD YOU CAN MAKE MONEY AT IT.

PERHAPS, BUT IT TAKES YEARS AND YEARS OF PRACTICE. YOU CAN'T JUST THINK YOU'LL IMMEDIATELY SELL SOMETHING.

TAKE IT FROM A LIFETIME STARVING ARTIST.
SOME GUY JUST OFFERED ME $500 FOR THIS.

AND WHAT'S THIS ONE CALLED?
"BITTER TURTLE"

MEGAN! I'VE DECIDED THAT WE SHOULD ALL TAKE A TRIP TO HONG KONG.
WONDERFUL IDEA!
YEAH. WE'LL TAKE A FAMILY VACATION TO SEE THE DRAGON BOAT RACES.
THE WHAT?
YOU MEAN, YOUR IDEA OF A FAMILY VACATION IS TO WATCH A SPORTING EVENT?
THERE'S MORE TO IT THAN THAT.
YOU CAN ALSO BET ON THEM.
OOH. RACING **AND** GAMBLING.
TRAVEL
YOU'RE COMING WITH US ON OUR TRIP TO HONG KONG?
I'M JOINING THIS EXPEDITION STRICTLY OUT OF SCIENTIFIC CURIOUSITY.
I WANT TO OBSERVE HOW A BOSSY CONTROL FREAK BEHAVES WHILE ON VACATION.
I'VE BEEN TOLD THAT A BOSSY CONTROL FREAK MIGHT BE JOINING US.
ALL SOFT LUGGAGE GOES THERE.

HERE WE ARE, MEGAN... THE ANNUAL DRAGONBOAT RACES.
THE ROWING TEAMS ARE WARMING UP. THE BOATS ARE BEING PREPARED. COMPETITION IS IN THE AIR.
THERE'S A FEELING MEN GET WHEN COMPETITION IS IN THE AIR, MEGAN. IT'S AN URGE TO...
SIT ON A COUCH AND WATCH?
YO! HOTDOG HERE!

Sherman's Lagoon
HEY, SHERM, THIS IS DAVE, MARK, AND WOODY. THEY'RE MY FRIENDS. DON'T EAT THEM. OKAY?
RIGHT.
SOMETIMES HIS SHARK INSTINCT GETS THE BETTER OF HIM. JUST KEEP REMINDING HIM YOU'RE MY FRIENDS. I'LL BE BACK IN A MINUTE.
OKAY.
I'VE NEVER BEEN SO CLOSE TO A REAL-LIVE SHARK BEFORE.
YEAH. I GUESS WE HAVE A REPUTATION.
YOU'RE DAVE. YOU'RE ERNEST'S FRIEND, AND I SHOULDN'T EAT YOU.
RIGHT.
WHAT ABOUT MARK?
SAME DEAL.

WHAT ARE THE ODDS ON RUSTBUCKET?
FIFTY TO ONE.
PUT ME DOWN FOR 500 HONG KONG DOLLARS.
YOU GOT IT.
HAWTHORNE, WHAT ARE YOU DOING?
PLAYING BOOKIE FOR THESE DRAGON BOAT RACES.
YOU'RE RUNNING AN ILLEGAL GAMBLING RING IN A COMMUNIST TERRITORY?
BOY, YOU CAN MAKE **ANYTHING** SOUND NEGATIVE.

SO, WHICH DRAGONBOAT DO YOU WANT TO BET ON TO WIN THE RACE?
STINKPOT.
STINKPOT?
I'M PICKING IT 'CUZ I LIKE THE NAME.
IT WAS MY NICKNAME IN HIGHSCHOOL.
MAKES REUNIONS DIFFICULT.

UH OH. I THINK I MADE A BASIC BOOKIE ERROR. AFTER THAT LAST RACE I SEEM TO OWE EVERYONE A LOT MORE MONEY THAN I COLLECTED. I MUST'VE CALCULATED THE ODDS WRONG.
I SEE YOUR PROBLEM. YOU FORGOT TO CARRY THE TWO RIGHT THERE.
OH YEAH. SILLY ME.
BUT NOW I'VE GOT ANOTHER PROBLEM.
WHAT'S THAT?
A HOARD OF ANGRY GAMBLERS ARE GOING TO TEAR ME TO SHREDS.
I ONLY DO MATH PROBLEMS.

GROSS. IT'S A FISH HEAD IN A BAG.
UH OH. IT'S A WARNING FROM THE CHINESE MAFIA. THEY'RE OUT TO GET US.
GREAT. NOT ONLY DO WE HAVE A HOARD OF IRATE GAMBLERS CHASING US, NOW THE CHINESE MAFIA IS INVOLVED. AND IT'S ALL YOUR FAULT.
AND ALL I WANTED TO DO WAS SEE SOME DRAGONBOAT RACES WITH THE FAMILY.
I'M GOING TO THINK TWICE BEFORE BRINGING YOU ALONG ON OUR NEXT VACATION.
CAN I BORROW YOUR TOOTHBRUSH?
HOME SWEET HOME.
THE DRAGONBOAT RACES WERE FUN. WE SHOULD ALL VACATION TOGETHER MORE OFTEN.
ARE YOU NUTS? YOU NEARLY GOT US ALL KILLED BY THE CHINESE MAFIA!
I'M SURE YOUR WIFE ISN'T THINKING SO NEGATIVELY.
THAT'S IT FOR CRAB RECIPES?
MAYBE IT'S OFF-SEASON.

IT'S YOUR MOTHER.
RING RING RING
HOW DO YOU KNOW?
MAYBE IT'S INTUITION, MAYBE IT'S A SIXTH SENSE.
RING RING
RING RING
MAYBE IT'S THE FACT THAT I JUST HUNG UP ON HER.
SHERMAN!
RING RING

SHERMAN'S LAGOON
CURRICULUM VITAE
SHERMAN T. SHARK
KAPUPU LAGOON
MICRONESIA
Employment History
Cartoon Shark, King Features Syndicate, 1991-present
I star in the syndicated comic strip Sherman's Lagoon
(www.shermanslagoon.com), which appears daily in over 200 North
newspapers, including the Washington Post, the Chicago Tribune, the
Francisco Chronicle, and the Toronto Star. The strip also
America, Europe, Australia and Asia in Swedish,
Estonian and Portuguese.
Pizza Chef, 1999
THE KEY TO GETTING AHEAD IN LIFE IS WRITING A GOOD RESUMÉ, SHERMAN. SO LET'S GET STARTED.
OKEY DOKE.
CURRENT POSITION?
SHARK.
JOB DESCRIPTION?
TAP TAP TAP
UM, I SWIM AROUND AND EAT STUFF.
WHAT MAKES YOU UNIQUELY QUALIFIED TO DO THIS?
TAP TAP TAP TAP TAP TAP
WELL, I'VE GOT A TAIL ON ONE END AND A MOUTH ON THE OTHER.
WHAT ASPECTS OF YOUR JOB DO YOU ENJOY THE MOST?
TAP TAP TAP
WELL, I LIKE EATING STUFF MORE THAN I LIKE SWIMMING AROUND, I GUESS.
RIGHT.
TAP TAP TAP TAP TAP
WHAT DO YOU SEE YOURSELF DOING TEN YEARS FROM NOW?
HMMMM...
I'D LIKE TO BE SITTING AROUND EATING STUFF.
A MANAGEMENT POSITION.
TAP TAP TAP

I TELL YA ERNEST, SOMETIMES I FEEL LIKE NOBODY LISTENS.
LIKE I MIGHT AS WELL BE TALKING TO MYSELF.
YOU EVER FEEL LIKE THAT?
ERNEST?
WHO ARE YOU TALKING TO?
YOU, NOW.

WHAT'S YOUR NAME? I'M OSCAR.
LOOK, OSCAR, I DON'T MEAN TO BE RUDE...
BUT I'M NOT GOING TO BE IN THIS KOI POND LONG ENOUGH TO GET TO KNOW YOU.
I'M SURE MY FRIENDS ARE IN FULL-BLOWN RESCUE MODE AS WE SPEAK.
DON'T WE USUALLY HAVE A FOURTH FOR POKER?
SOMETHING'S MISSING.

ERNEST STILL IS MISSING.
WHEN WAS THE LAST TIME YOU SAW HIM?
WE WUZ TALKIN' YESTERDAY, AND HE JUST DISAPPEARED.
THAT'S ODD.
WHERE'D HE GO TO?
MAYBE HE RAN IN FEAR OF BAD GRAMMAR.
NAH. HE AIN'T LIKE THAT.

WHATCHA DOIN'?
PUTTING UP SOME POSTERS.
ERNEST SEEMS TO HAVE DISAPPEARED, AND I'M PRETTY UPSET ABOUT IT. IT'S BECOME MY ENTIRE FOCUS RIGHT NOW.
"MY BEST FRIEND HAS GONE MISSING. I FEAR THE WORST. IF YOU HAVE ANY INFORMATION, PLEASE CALL 555-1299."
"ALSO: USED GUITAR FOR SALE."
WHILE I HAVE YOUR ATTENTION.
GUYS! WE'VE GOT TO RESCUE ERNEST! I JUST TALKED TO A SEAGULL WHO SAYS HE SAW HIM!
ERNEST IS IN A KOI POND JUST INLAND.
WELL, IF WE WANT TO ATTEMPT A RESCUE, WE'LL NEED A PLAN.
AND WHAT'S THE MOST IMPORTANT THING ABOUT FORMING A RESCUE PLAN?
COOL CODE NAMES!
EXACTLY! I'LL BE RED LEADER ONE!

DOESN'T LOOK LIKE YOUR FRIENDS ARE COMING TO RESCUE YOU.
FACE IT. YOU'RE GOING TO BE STUCK IN THIS KOI POND FOR THE DURATION.
THEY'LL BE HERE!
I'M SURE IT'S SOME IMPORTANT DETAIL OF THE RESCUE PLAN THAT THEY'RE WORKING OUT.
VERTICAL OR HORIZONTAL CAMOUFLAGE STRIPES?
DOES THIS WALKIE TALKIE MAKE ME LOOK FAT?

SHERMAN'S LAG
HOW'S THE LIVE GIANT SQUID?
MENU
VERY PEPPY.
I'LL TRY IT.
MENU
A FINE CHOICE, MONSIEUR.
MENU
LIVE GIANT SQUID?
WHY NOT?
WHEN YOU COME TO ONE OF THESE FANCY-SCHMANCY RESTAURANTS YOU MIGHT AS WELL ORDER SOMETHING EXOTIC.
YOUR SQUID FORK, MONSIEUR.
WELL, THIS OUGHT TO BE INTERESTING.
SHOULD'VE GOTTEN THE SPAGHETTI.

OKAY, YOU TWO WILL HAVE TO SCALE THAT JAGGED CLIFF TO RESCUE ERNEST.
WHADDAYA MEAN "WE TWO"? AREN'T YOU COMING ALONG?
I CAN'T CLIMB.
AND BESIDES, IT'S NOT LIKE WHAT I'LL BE DOING IS WITHOUT RISK!
WHICH IS?
THE "JUMBLE" IN PEN.
THERE'S THE KOI POND!
HEY! THERE'S ERNEST!
ERNEST! YOU OKAY?
FILLMORE! HAWTHORNE! I KNEW YOU GUYS WOULD COME!
GET ME OUT OF THIS PLACE! LET'S GO HOME!
WHOA... CHECK OUT THE DIGS.
HAWTHORNE! THERE'S NO TIME TO STEAL STUFF!
NOT WITH YOU SCREAMING LIKE THAT!
GREAT RESCUE PLAN! I CAN'T CLIMB DOWN A CLIFF!
IF WE FLING YOU FAR ENOUGH OUT, YOU'RE GOING TO HIT THE WATER WITH A BIG SPLASH. DON'T WORRY.
AUUGHHH!
... MAYBE ON THE SECOND BOUNCE.
HAD TO HURT.

HOW LONG ARE YOU IN THE BODY CAST FOR?
COUPLE WEEKS.
THE DOCTORS HERE AT THE SMALL FISH CLINIC SAID YOU'RE LUCKY TO BE ALIVE AT ALL.
WHAT'S MY CHART SAY?
THEY HAVE YOU DOWN AS A "POSSIBLE FLUSHER."
THAT'S AN IMPROVEMENT.
OH GREAT KAHUNA, ALL KNOWING, ALL SEEING...
I COME TO YOU SEEKING ADVICE.
AGAIN?
SHOULD I PROCEED WITH THE PATH THAT I HAVE RECENTLY CHOSEN OR CALL IT QUITS?
KAHUNA SAY "GO FOR IT."
ANOTHER LONG POTTY BREAK?
I'M ALL IN.

HERE YOU GO, BOYS. FLYERS FOR MY NEW BUSINESS VENTURE.
"THE LOVING CLAW DAY CARE CENTER"? YOU DON'T EVEN **LIKE** KIDS.
SURE I DO!
THEY'RE SWEET AND SMALL AND ROUND...
THOSE ARE M&M'S.
WELL, AS LONG AS NOTHING MELTS IN MY HAND, I'LL BE ALL RIGHT.

Sherman's Lagoon
HERE'S A PHOTO OF HERMAN ASLEEP IN HIS HIGH CHAIR. ISN'T HE CUTE?
YEAH, WHATEVER.
EVERY PARENT THINKS THEIR KID IS THE CUTEST THING IN THE WORLD.
GROUCH.
SOMEDAY WHEN YOU HAVE KIDS, YOU'LL FEEL THE SAME WAY.
TAKE COVER!
AUGH!
OW!
OW!
OOH!
OUCH!
OW!
OUCH!
AUGH!
OOH!
OW!
OW!
OOH!
YOU OKAY?
I THINK SO.
AREN'T THEY THE CUTEST?
YEAH, WHATEVER.

HOW'S THE NEW DAYCARE BUSINESS, HAWTHORNE?
GOING LIKE GANG BUSTERS.
Hawthorne's Daycare
SAY, WOULD YOU LIKE TO WORK FOR ME?
Hawthorne Daycare
ME? SURE, WHY NOT?
GREAT. THIS WAY.
HEY KIDS! I GOT YOU A TRAMPOLINE!
WHERE?

SHERMAN HERE, REPORTING FOR WORK.
FINALLY!
Hawthorne's Daycare
HERE AT THE DAYCARE CENTER WE START WORK AT SIX A.M.! THAT'S WHEN THE KIDS START GETTING DROPPED OFF.
THAT'S AWFUL EARLY FOR ME.
MAYBE I COULD WORK THE NIGHT SHIFT.
IT'S DAYCARE!
Hawthorne's Daycare

SEE THAT DIAPER PAIL?
WHEN OPENED, THAT DIAPER PAIL IS CAPABLE OF RENDERING THE HARDIEST SOUL UNCONSCIOUS.
EMPTYING THAT DIAPER PAIL IS NOT A FEAT FOR THE FAINT OF HEART, SHERMAN.
AND THAT'S WHY I HAVE EMPLOYEES. HAVE AT IT.
I WANT HAZARD PAY!

I NEED TO DROP CLAYTON OFF. I'VE GOT A BRUNCH DATE WITH A SHE-TURTLE.
Hawthorne's Daycare
AND SHE'S HOT.
WHAT ARE YOU DOING.
COVERING HIS EARS.
WE TRY NOT TO LIE IN FRONT OF THE KIDS.
JUST TAKE CARE OF HIM.
SHERMAN, SINCE THIS IS YOUR FIRST DAY ON THE JOB, LET ME EXPLAIN THE CONCEPT OF NAPTIME.
Hawthorne's Daycare
NAPTIME IS THE TIME OF DAY I LOOK FORWARD TO MOST HERE AT THE DAYCARE CENTER.
FOR TWO WONDERFUL HOURS I GET SOME RELIEF FROM THESE SCREAMING RUGRATS. MY WORLD BECOMES TRANQUIL AGAIN. THAT'S WHAT NAPTIME IS ABOUT.
SOUNDS WONDERFUL.
SO, WAKE ME UP IN TWO HOURS.
HEY!

WHAT HAPPENED TO YOUR DAYCARE BUSINESS?
I GOT SHUT DOWN.
CLOSED

APPARENTLY, ONE NEEDS A "LICENSE" TO OPERATE A DAYCARE CENTER.
CLOSED

BOY, YOU NEED A LICENSE TO DO ANYTHING THESE DAYS.
CLOSED

IT'S LIKE WHEN YOU WERE A SURGEON ALL OVER AGAIN.
EXACTLY!
CLOSED

YOU'RE BACK. GOOD. DID YOU GET EVERYTHING I PUT ON THE GROCERY LIST?
MORE OR LESS.
THIS ISN'T THE BRAND OF PAPER TOWELS I ASKED FOR.
I THOUGHT THEY WERE ALL THE SAME.
THEY'RE NOT ALL THE SAME.
BOY, PICKY PICKY.
AND YOU JUST GRABBED THE FIRST BOX OF DETERGENT YOU SAW, DIDN'T YOU?
YOU'RE TELLING ME THERE'S A DIFFERENCE IN DETERGENTS, TOO?
YES!!
I SHOULD NEVER SEND A MAN TO THE GROCERY STORE.
DON'T WE ALREADY HAVE BEER?
THIS IS AFTER-DINNER BEER.

I'LL DO YOU A GAME OF "CLAW-FIN" FOR THE LAST SLICE OF PIZZA.
YOU'RE ON!
OKAY. ONE, TWO, THREE, GO!
CLAW BEATS FIN. IT'S MINE.
MAN! IT'S LIKE YOU WIN EVERY TIME WE DO THAT!
OKAY, HERMAN, THIS IS AN IMPORTANT LESSON... PAY ATTENTION.
SOMETIMES YOU'LL WANT A PEANUT BUTTER AND JELLY SANDWICH, BUT THEN YOU'LL DISCOVER THERE'S NO JELLY.
IN THIS SITUATION, MARSHMELLOW CREAM CAN BE SUBSTITUTED.
SHERMAN! WHAT ARE YOU DOING?
RAISING A SURVIVOR! THANK YOU!

SHERMAN, WE NEED TO DO SOMETHING ABOUT OUR CURRENT SITUATION.
AGREED, WHATEVER IT IS.
WE'RE BOTH TOO BUSY BETWEEN WORK AND RAISING HERMAN TO KEEP THIS PLACE CLEAN.
YEP.
SO, ARE YOU THINKING WHAT I'M THINKING?
I DON'T SEE ANY OTHER SOLUTION.
ABANDON THIS LAGOON AND FIND A CLEAN ONE?
HIRE SOME HELP.

HERE'S OUR FIRST BUTLER APPLICANT.
HEY, I'M TED.
HI, TED... YOU'RE A BUTLER?
NOT CURRENTLY.
WELL, WHAT ARE YOU CURRENTLY?
JUST A DUDE STANDING HERE.
I LIKE HIS HONESTY.
NEXT!

SHERMAN, THIS PLACE IS STILL A MESS! DIDN'T YOU SAY YOU WOULD FIND US SOME DOMESTIC HELP?
PIZZ
SODA

SINCE WHEN HAS IT BEEN MY JOB TO HIRE THE HELP AROUND HERE, MEGAN?
SINCE YOU SAID YOU WOULD!

SINCE WHEN HAVE I EVER BEEN RELIABLE?
OH, NO YOU DON'T!

MEGAN AND I ARE THINKING OF GETTING A BUTLER.
WHY?

WE'RE TOO BUSY. NEITHER OF US HAS TIME TO CLEAN.

YET YOU HAVE TIME TO GOLF WHENEVER IT'S SUGGESTED.
YEAH. WEIRD, HUH?

SHERMAN'S

SHERMAN, COME HERE. I WANT TO SHOW YOU SOMETHING.

WHAT?
ONE OF THESE CREAMS IS FOR DRY SKIN AND THE OTHER IS FOR DIAPER RASH.

DO YOU KNOW THE DIFFERENCE?

NO.
I THOUGHT SO.

THIS ONE IS FOR DIAPER RASH. GOT IT?

GOT IT.
NOW, WOULD YOU CALL THIS A CASE OF DRY SKIN OR DIAPER RASH?

IS THIS A TEST? CUZ I DON'T MIND FLUNKING.
KIDS THESE DAYS.

WELL, JEEVES, WELCOME ABOARD.
THANK YOU, SIR.
MEGAN AND I HAVE NEVER HAD A BUTLER BEFORE.
SO, UH... HOW'S THIS WORK?
IS THERE AN ON/OFF SWITCH BACK HERE?
PLEASE STOP THAT.
WOW, JEEVES! THE KITCHEN LOOKS FANTASTIC!
THANK YOU, MADAM.
THE SPICES ARE IN ALPHABETICAL ORDER, AND THE POTS ARE ALL ARRANGED BY SIZE...
YOU DIDN'T HAVE TIME TO TACKLE THAT NASTY FRIDGE, DID YOU?
BUT OF COURSE.
WHERE'D ALL THOSE ANCIENT LEFTOVERS GO?
MOST MADE A BREAK FOR IT.

SO, WHAT'VE YOU BEEN UP TO, JEEVES?
CATEGORIZING YOUNG MASTER HERMAN'S TOYS.

THEY ARE NOW IN BINS OF EDUCATIONAL, RECREATIONAL AND MUSICAL.
HOLY SCHMOKES.

I'VE TAKEN THE LIBERTY OF CATEGORIZING MASTER SHERMAN'S THINGS AS WELL.
WHAT THINGS?

SALTY, CHOCOLATEY, AND RANCH FLAVORED.
AWESOME.

BOY, JEEVES WHIPPED OUR HOUSE INTO SHAPE IN ONLY TWO DAYS.
HE'S GREAT.
MAKES ME FEEL PRETTY LAZY FOR ALL THE TIME I DIDN'T DO IT.
THERE'S NOT A LOT OF NEED TO KEEP HIM AROUND.
HEY! I'M FINDING THINGS FOR HIM TO DO!
FINISHED YOUR SODUKU PUZZLE, SIR.
YES! IN RECORD TIME!
JEEVES, WE JUST DON'T...
HAVE ENOUGH FOR ME TO DO.
RIGHT. SO I'M AFRAID WE'RE GOING TO HAVE TO...
LET ME GO.
MAN, YOU ARE EFFICIENT.
THE "GOOD LUCK" CARD YOU'D LIKE TO GIVE ME.
OOH! LET'S SEE WHAT I WROTE!

YO, CHECK OUT MY NEW CELL PHONE. THIS BABY'S LOADED.
CAMERA, INTERNET, RINGTONES, GAMES, TEXT MESSAGING, MUSIC, MOVIES...
CAN I BORROW IT? I NEED TO MAKE A PHONE CALL.
I GUESS.
SEEMS LIKE A SILLY THING TO USE A CELL PHONE FOR.
HELLO?

SHERMAN'S LAGOON
Select
Erase
Save
Transfer
Obfuscate
Panic
WE SHOULD DO THIS MORE OFTEN.
WHY DON'T WE GET A PHOTO?
LAGOON POTLUCK PICNIC
EVERYBODY HOLD STILL AND SMILE.
HANG ON. IT'S IN POWER SAVER MODE. DARN DIGITAL CAMERAS. OKAY, NOW SMILE.
WAIT. NOW I HAVE IT ON THE WRONG SETTING. OKAY, SMILE.
RATS. OUT OF MEMORY. LEMME ERASE A COUPLE PICTURES... NOW SMILE.
UH-OH. I'M GETTING A FLASHING RED LIGHT. HOLD ON... HERE'S THE PROBLEM. OKAY, SMILE.
THERE. NOW WE'VE PRESERVED THIS MOMENT OF HAPPINESS FOR POSTERITY.
CLICK!

WHY DID WE COME HERE, MEGAN? YOU KNOW I HATE ART GALLERIES.
OH, COME ON, SHERMAN. GIVE ART A CHANCE.
I MUST SAY, THIS PIECE MOVES ME. BUT, I LACK THE ELOQUENCE TO ADEQUATELY DESCRIBE THE FEELINGS I HAVE.
I'M FEELING MOVED, MEGAN.
IN THIS DIRECTION.
JUST GO.
MEN'S ROOM

WHEN YOU COME TO AN ART GALLERY, SHERMAN, YOU HAVE TO COME WITH AN OPEN MIND. ANYTHING CAN BE ART.
YOU HAVE TO LOOK AT EACH PIECE AND TRY TO CONNECT SOME PART OF YOUR LIFE TO IT. WHAT DOES THIS REMIND YOU OF?
GOOD HEAVENS! IT'S CARL THE CARP! HE'S BEEN FILLETED! IT'S MURDER MOST FOUL RIGHT HERE IN THIS MUSEUM!
HAVE YOU SEEN "THE DAVINCI CODE"?
OH, YOO HOO! GUARD!

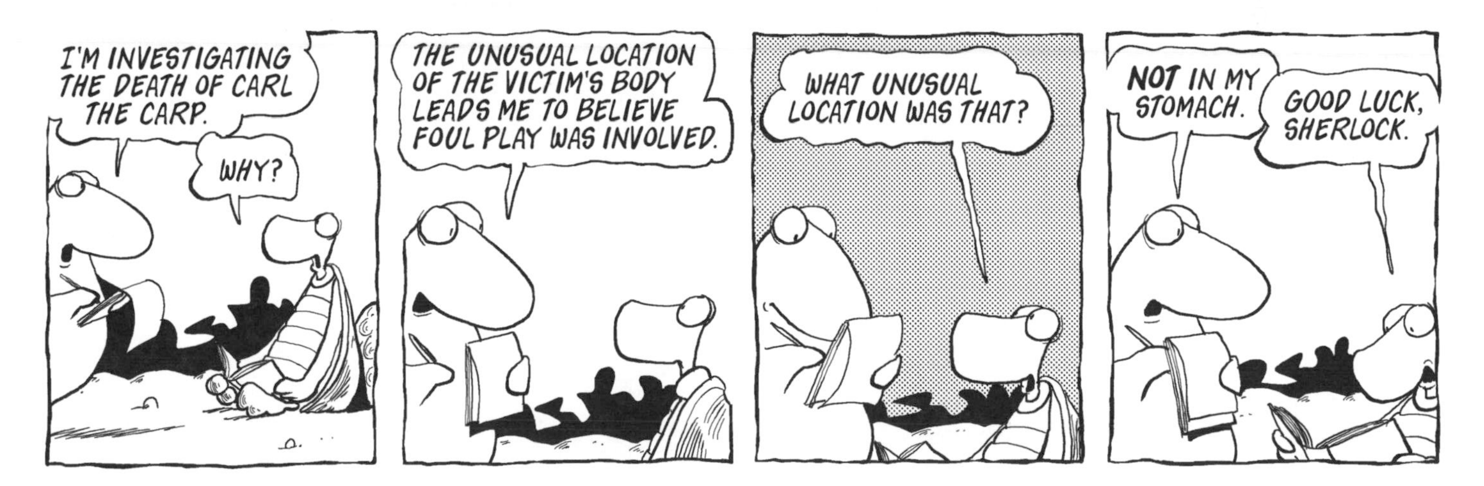

I'M INVESTIGATING THE DEATH OF CARL THE CARP.
WHY?
THE UNUSUAL LOCATION OF THE VICTIM'S BODY LEADS ME TO BELIEVE FOUL PLAY WAS INVOLVED.
WHAT UNUSUAL LOCATION WAS THAT?
NOT IN MY STOMACH.
GOOD LUCK, SHERLOCK.

STILL HUNG UP ABOUT THE DEATH OF CARL THE CARP?
SOMETHING'S FISHY ABOUT IT.
I'M REALLY GOING TO HAVE TO PUT ON MY PRIVATE EYE HAT FOR THIS ONE.
THAT'S A RAINBOW WIG.
I'M UNDER COVER.
HAWTHORNE, I'VE BEEN DIGGING INTO CARL'S MURDER, AND I'VE DISCOVERED SIGNS OF A SECRET SOCIETY RIGHT HERE IN THIS LAGOON!
NO!
YOU AREN'T A MEMBER ARE YOU?
NO!
YOU AREN'T LYING TO ME, ARE YOU?
NO!
YOU AREN'T LYING ABOUT LYING, ARE YOU?
YES!
LET'S START OVER.
NO!

I NEED TO ASK YOU SOME QUESTIONS ABOUT THE DEATH OF CARL THE CARP.
FIRE AWAY, SHERLOCK.
ARE YOU, OR HAVE YOU EVER BEEN, A MEMBER OF THE SECRET SOCIETY KNOWN AS "OPUS SESAME"?
HUH?
IT'S TRUE! I CAN TELL BY YOUR REACTION!
LOOK THROUGH MY WALLET! I'VE GOT NOTHING TO HIDE!
BARRY MANILOW FAN CLUB?
WELL, ONE THING TO HIDE.

SHERMAN'S LAGOON
STILL HUNG UP ABOUT YOUR CAREER PATH, BRUCE?
I THINK I'VE HAD A BREAK-THROUGH.
REALLY?
YEAH. YOU KNOW, IT'S ALL ABOUT LISTENING TO THE CALL OF DESTINY.
AND, WHAT DID DESTINY SAY?
DESTINY SAID LOOK IN THE MIRROR FOR THE ANSWER.
SO I DID. AND THAT'S WHEN IT HIT ME. I'M UNIQUE.
I WAS BORN TO DO ONE THING, AND I SHOULDN'T FIGHT IT ANYMORE.
I WAS BORN TO BE... A FASHION MODEL.
I THOUGHT YOU WERE GOING TO SAY "HEDGE TRIMMER."
REALLY?

SHERMAN, LET ME HELP IN YOUR MURDER INVESTIGATION.
I DON'T KNOW, ERNEST. THIS PROBABLY ISN'T A PLACE FOR KIDS.
I'M DISCOVERING SECRET SOCIETIES AND ALL KINDS OF NEFARIOUS ACTIVITY. I CAN'T GUARANTEE YOUR SAFETY.
I'LL BRING DOUGHNUTS.
WE START EACH MORNING AT NINE-ISH.

MAYBE THIS SECRET SOCIETY IS SO SECRET THAT YOU'RE A MEMBER AND YOU DON'T EVEN KNOW IT.
MAYBE SO.
HAVE YOU TAKEN A CLOSE LOOK AT YOUR FINANCES LATELY?
NO.
PERHAPS YOU'RE PAYING DUES TO AN ORGANIZATION YOU JOINED LONG AGO WHEN YOU WERE YOUNG AND FOOLISH.
YES.
AND NOW, YEARS LATER, YOU WONDER WHY YOU'RE A MEMBER, OR IF IT EVEN EXISTS.
MY HEALTH CLUB.

LOOK WHAT I'VE DISCOVERED ABOUT THIS SECRET "OPUS SESAME" SOCIETY.
ONE OF THEIR RITUALS INVOLVES INTENTIONAL PAIN AND SUFFERING.
YOU MEAN?
THAT'S RIGHT.
THEY'RE CUBS FANS.
SCARY.

I THINK I'VE FOUND THE CAUSE OF CARL'S DEATH... IT'S...
UGH!
FWAP!
SHERMAN, ARE YOU OKAY?
ALL IN A DAY'S WORK FOR A PRIVATE EYE. NOW THE KILLER'S AFTER ME.
FEELS LIKE... A LARGE-CALIBER BULLET.
NOPE.
IT'S A TITLEIST FROM HAWTHORNE.
CAN I GET A RULING ON THIS?
WELL, I'VE SOLVED THE MYSTERY OF THE MURDER OF CARL THE CARP.
WAS IT SOMEONE WE KNOW?
UH, NO.
WAS IT THAT SECRETIVE CULT, OPUS SESAME?
AGAIN, NO.
IT WAS A FISHERMAN NAMED ROGER.
NATURAL CAUSES.
SO, YOU'RE THAT NEW SPECIES OF SHARK, HUH? HOW LONG HAS THIS SPECIES BEEN AROUND?
NOT LONG. WE KEEP EVOLVING WITH THE TIMES. GOTTA STAY AHEAD, YA KNOW.
WELL, MY KIND OF SHARK HAS ADAPTED TO MODERNITY, TOO.
I JUST GOT CABLE.
I'VE JUST GROWN A DISH.

SHERMAN'S

I'M OFF TO HOLLYWOOD TO GET MY OWN TV SHOW.
YEAH, RIGHT.

HEY, IF SPONGEBOB CAN DO IT, WHY CAN'T I?

SPONGES ARE SOFT AND CUDDLY. CRABS ARE HARD AND POINTY.

AND THEY LIVE IN DARK LITTLE HOLES AND FEED ON GARBAGE.

BESIDES, CRABS HAVE NO TALENT.

YOU'RE NO SPONGE, YOU'RE A SCOURING PAD... AN OBNOXIOUS, TALENTLESS SCOURING PAD.

HMPH!
ER

TIME FOR ANOTHER EPISODE OF "HAWTHORNE THE OBNOXIOUS TALENTLESS SCOURING PAD."
NOT INTERESTED.

NEED ANY HELP IN THE KITCHEN, MEGAN?
THANKS. YOU KNOW, THE MALE GREAT WHITE SHARK WON'T GO NEAR THE KITCHEN.
ACTUALLY, WITH MY SPECIES, THE MALE COOKS, CLEANS, AND GIVES THE FEMALES NECK RUBS.
WHAT WAS THAT FOR?
WHACK!
SO, WHAT ELSE MAKES YOUR SPECIES DIFFERENT FROM OTHER SHARKS?
WELL...
THROUGH TIME WE'VE BECOME TRIMMER AND MORE AERODYNAMIC.
WE CAN CUT THROUGH THE WATER MUCH MORE EFFICIENTLY.
IS THAT A RACING STRIPE?
OPTIONAL.

SO, WHAT'S UP WITH THAT NEW SPECIES OF SHARK HANGING AROUND THE LAGOON?
OH, MAN!
HE'S LIKE SOME GENETICALLY SUPERIOR BEING. EVOLUTION'S BEEN VERY GOOD TO HIM.
AW, C'MON. GREAT WHITE SHARKS MUST'VE HAD SOME REMARKABLE EVOLUTIONARY DEVELOPMENTS THROUGH TIME.
WELL, THERE IS THE TWINKIE POUCH.
DO YOU EVER CLEAN THAT THING?

WELL, I BETTER GET GOING.
BUT YOU JUST GOT HERE!
AS A NEWLY DISCOVERED SPECIES OF SHARK, I'VE GOT A LOT GOING ON... INTERVIEWS, PHOTO SHOOTS, CASE STUDIES.
OUR LIVES ARE PLENTY EXCITING AS WELL.
CAN YOU HIT MY BACK WITH SOME ACNE CREAM?

ENERGY IS THE WORD OF THE DAY, FAT BOY. THE WORLD NEEDS MORE OF IT. THERE'S MONEY TO BE MADE.
HOW?
BY TAPPING INTO NEW ENERGY SOURCES... HYDRO, WIND, NUKE, NATURAL GAS...
NATURAL GAS?
AND I'VE BEEN GIVING IT AWAY ALL THIS TIME.
WE'VE TRIED TO DISCOURAGE THAT.

SO, ARE THESE YOUR PLANS FOR A NEW ENERGY SOURCE FOR THE LAGOON?
YEP.
HOW'S IT WORK?
FILLMORE, I'M IN THE MIDDLE OF CREATING TECHNICAL SPECIFICATIONS. I DON'T HAVE TIME TO EXPLAIN THIS STUFF TO A LAYMAN.
WHAT'S THE TWIRLY THING DO?
"TWIRLY THING"... THAT'S THE TERM I WAS LOOKING FOR.

SHERMAN'S LAGOON
DOESN'T THE DELICATE BALANCE OF NATURE AMAZE YOU?
UM... HOW SO?
SEE THAT LITTLE FISH? IT KNOWS IT MUST SWIM A TINY BIT FASTER THAN THE BIGGER FISH, OR IT WILL BE EATEN.
AND THE BIGGER FISH KNOWS IT MUST SWIM A TINY BIT FASTER THAN THE LITTLE FISH, OR IT WILL STARVE.
DAY AFTER DAY, THIS COMPLEX LITTLE DRAMA PLAYS OUT IN OUR VERY LAGOON.
USED TO WORK LIKE THAT. NOT ANYMORE.
AUGH!
ZZZZZZZZZZ
WHERE'D HE GET THAT?
EBAY.

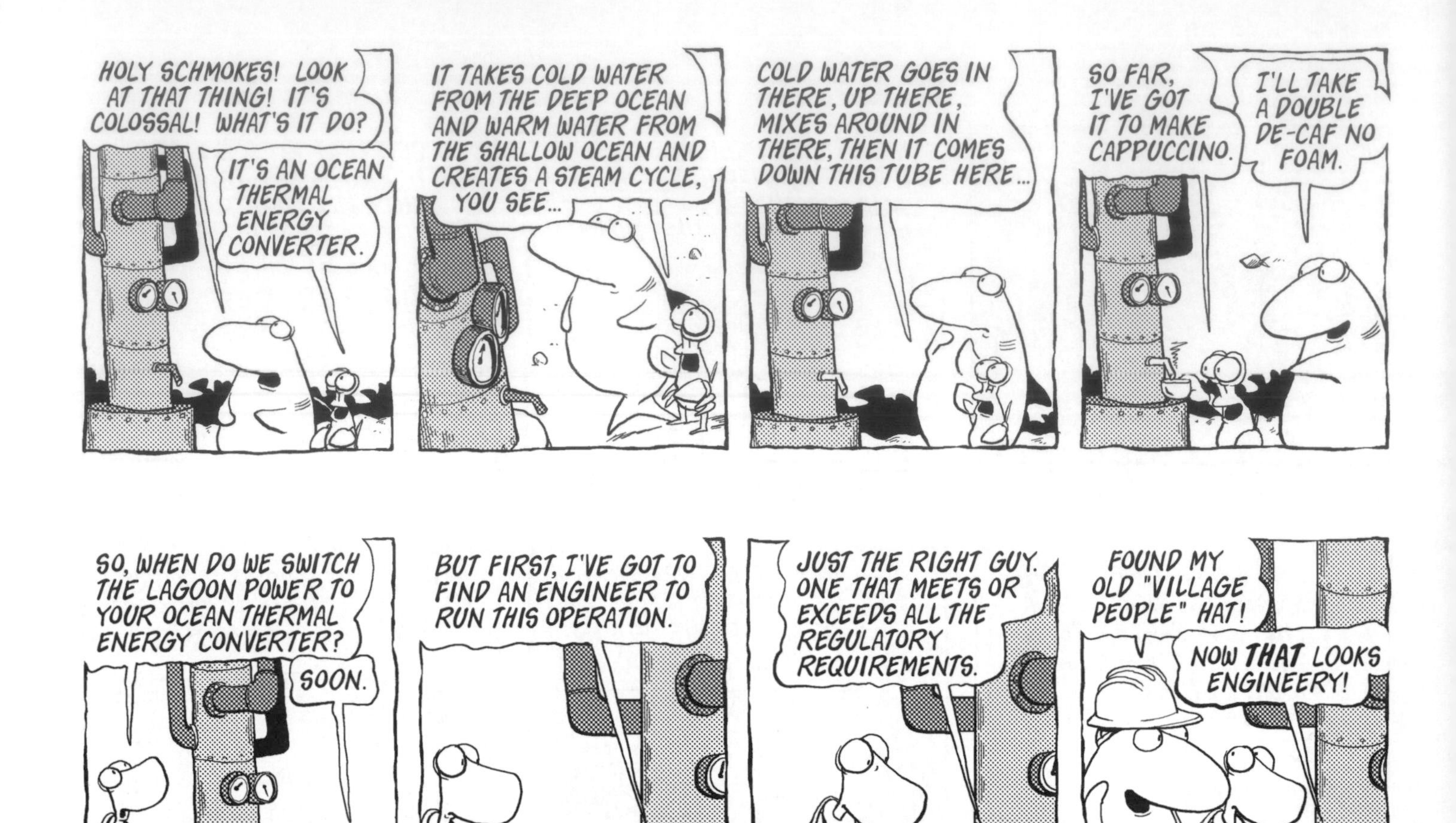
HOLY SCHMOKES! LOOK AT THAT THING! IT'S COLOSSAL! WHAT'S IT DO?
IT'S AN OCEAN THERMAL ENERGY CONVERTER.
IT TAKES COLD WATER FROM THE DEEP OCEAN AND WARM WATER FROM THE SHALLOW OCEAN AND CREATES A STEAM CYCLE, YOU SEE...
COLD WATER GOES IN THERE, UP THERE, MIXES AROUND IN THERE, THEN IT COMES DOWN THIS TUBE HERE...
SO FAR, I'VE GOT IT TO MAKE CAPPUCCINO.
I'LL TAKE A DOUBLE DE-CAF NO FOAM.
SO, WHEN DO WE SWITCH THE LAGOON POWER TO YOUR OCEAN THERMAL ENERGY CONVERTER?
SOON.
BUT FIRST, I'VE GOT TO FIND AN ENGINEER TO RUN THIS OPERATION.
JUST THE RIGHT GUY. ONE THAT MEETS OR EXCEEDS ALL THE REGULATORY REQUIREMENTS.
FOUND MY OLD "VILLAGE PEOPLE" HAT!
NOW THAT LOOKS ENGINEERY!

SHERMAN, AS CHIEF ENGINEER OF MY OCEAN THERMAL ENERGY CONVERTER...
...YOU'LL NEED TO KNOW ALL THE WORKINGS AND INTRICACIES OF THIS OPERATION.
ON AND OFF?
PRETTY MUCH.

ARE WE READY TO POWER UP THIS BABY?
READY!
THE FLIP OF THIS SWITCH IS GOING TO USHER IN A NEW ERA OF RENEWABLE ENERGY FOR THE LAGOON!
ZAP!
LISTEN, CREEP. DON'T "LIGHTS OUT ON THE COUCH" ME OUR FIRST DATE!
I DIDN'T TOUCH ANYTHING!
I'LL BET YOU'RE WONDERING WHAT THAT POWER FAILURE WAS ALL ABOUT LAST NIGHT.
NOPE.
IT JUST SO HAPPENS I'M IN THE PROCESS OF REVOLUTIONIZING THE WAY WE GENERATE ENERGY AROUND HERE.
AND WE HIT A LITTLE BUMP IN THE ROAD TO THE FUTURE, THAT'S ALL.
YOU SEE, I'M AN IDEAS MAN.
ANY IDEAS ON HOW TO GET ME OUT OF THIS CONVERSATION?
okay, fillmore, knight to king's bishop three.
TAP TAP TAP
AAUUGH! ANOTHER STUPID POWER OUTAGE!
ZAP!
WELL, LOOKS LIKE WE CAN'T PLAY INTERNET CHESS.
WE COULD ALWAYS PLAY THE OLD FASHIONED WAY.
SO, HOW DO THESE THINGS MOVE. ARE THEY BATTERY POWERED?
THINK OF IT AS EXERCISE.

SHERMAN'S LAGOON

DO WE HAVE ALL THE BABY STUFF?
FORGOT THE DIAPERS.

ANYTHING ELSE?
NOPE. LET'S GO.

DID YOU BRING HERMAN'S TOY?
NO. I THOUGHT YOU PACKED IT.

OKAY. GOT THE TOY. ANYTHING ELSE?
NO. LET'S GO.

THE FOLDING CRIB!
HOW COULD WE FORGET THAT?

OKAY. DO WE HAVE EVERYTHING NOW?
WE HAVE EVERYTHING. LET'S GO.

FORGOT THE BABY.
LET'S JUST STAY IN.

HAWTHORNE, THIS RENEWABLE ENERGY EXPERIMENT OF YOURS IS A COMPLETE BUST.
YEAH, YEAH, I KNOW.
TAPPING INTO THE LAGOON'S THERMAL ENERGY JUST ISN'T WORKING.
I'LL SHIFT US BACK TO THE OLD ENERGY SOURCE.
WHAT **WAS** THE OLD ENERGY SOURCE?
TAPPING INTO THE BAYSIDE HILTON.
WOULDN'T A FIREPLACE BE ROMANTIC?
MEGAN, WE'RE UNDERWATER. IT'S NOT POSSIBLE.
CAN YOU JUST AGREE THAT THE **IDEA** OF A FIREPLACE WOULD BE ROMANTIC?
DO I HAVE TO CHOP WOOD IN THIS IDEA?
FORGET IT, PLEASE.
ANOTHER EIGHT! I HATE THIS GAME!
YOU JUST NEED TO WORK ON YOUR PUTTING.
AND YOUR DRIVING.
AND YOUR SHORT GAME.
IS THERE ANY PART OF THIS GAME I'M GOOD AT?
YOUR CUSSING'S SHOWN IMPROVEMENT.

WHAT'S THIS? ANOTHER SCHEME OF YOURS TO TURN A QUICK BUCK?
IT'S THE SWINGMASTER 5000. GUARANTEED TO IMPROVE YOUR GOLF SWING.
Swingmaster 5000
JUST WHAT THE WORLD NEEDS- ANOTHER GOLF GADGET.
GOLFERS ARE ETERNAL OPTIMISTS.
THEY'RE ALWAYS WILLING TO TRY SOME NEW THING TO IMPROVE THEIR GAME.
AND YOU'RE SELLING THEM THEIR OWN FANTASY. SHAME ON YOU.
YOU KNOW, THIS COULD HELP YOU MEET WOMEN.
I'LL TAKE ONE.

YOU SELLING ANY OF THESE?
YEAH. AND I HAVEN'T EVEN ADVERTISED YET.
Swingmaster 5000
I JUST NEED SOME REALLY BAD GOLFER SO I CAN SHOOT A SALES VIDEO.
FORE!
Swingmaster 5000
I'M HOT TODAY.
A STAR IS BORN.
Swingmaster 5000

CAN THIS THING REALLY HELP MY GOLF GAME?
WHAT WAS YOUR LAST SCORE?
Swingmaster 5000
only $29.95
79.
ON NINE OR EIGHTEEN HOLES?
Swingmaster 5000
only $29.95
only $29.95
JUST GIVE ME ONE.
SAY NO MORE.
Swingmaster 5000

SHERMAN'S LAGOON
AUGH! I'M GOING TO DIE!!
HUH?
I JUST DISCOVERED THIS RED SPOT ON MY FIN, SO I GOOGLED "RED SPOT" AND LOOK!
I COULD HAVE ANY ONE OF THESE DISEASES. OR ALL OF THEM SIMULTANEOUSLY!
Carnivore Weekly
HERE'S A CHAT ROOM FOR PEOPLE WITH RED SPOTS. (SNIFF) I LOVE YOU ALL.
WOW. I CAN BUY A BOOK ABOUT RED SPOTS. MAYBE I SHOULD GET A BOOK TO BETTER UNDERSTAND MY AFFLICTION.
WHAT'S THIS LINK?
HMMM.
THAT'S A GOOD DEAL ON THE RED-SPOTTED BLOUSE.
YOU CAN'T TAKE IT WITH YOU.

HERE GOES MY FIRST SHOT WITH THE PATENTED SWINGMASTER 5000.
UNGH!
I'D SAY YOU GAINED SOME DISTANCE ON THAT DRIVE.
STRAIGHT AS AN ARROW, TOO.

WHOOOWEE, THAT'S A BIG YACHT.
A REAL HUMDINGER.

THAT GUY MUST HAVE A LOT OF MONEY. I'M HAPPY FOR HIM. HE'S A TRIBUTE TO THE HUMAN SPIRIT.
YES, HE IS.

HE JUST HIT A ROCK.
GOOD.

DID YOU SEE THAT BIG YACHT THAT SANK IN THE LAGOON? SOME RICH GUY RAN IT INTO A ROCK.

COME ON, WHAT AN IDIOT! I MEAN, HOW DUMB DO YOU HAVE TO BE TO JUST RUN INTO A ...

WHAM!

YOU WERE SAYING?
PIERS ARE DIFFERENT. THEY SNEAK UP ON YOU.

WELCOME TO MY SUNKEN YACHT, BOYS.
YOUR SUNKEN YACHT?
THAT'S RIGHT. I WAS HERE FIRST. FINDERS KEEPERS.
"FINDERS KEEPERS"? THAT'S THE MOST MATURE SYSTEM YOU CAN COME UP WITH?
YOU GOT SOMETHING BETTER?
EENY MEENY...
IT WON'T HOLD UP IN COURT!!
BOY, WHOEVER OWNED THIS YACHT HAD TERRIBLE TASTE.
YOU THINK SO?
YEAH. LOOK AT SOME OF THIS ARTWORK.
WHAT KIND OF TACKY CHEESEBALL KNUCKLEHEAD WOULD BUY A PAINTING OF...
HEY! AN ELVIS ON VELVET! JUST LIKE MINE!
ASKED AND ANSWERED.

FILLMORE! PUT ON YOUR SHELL!
IN A MINUTE.
I CAN'T FULLY ENJOY THIS MASSAGE CHAIR WITH MY SHELL ON.
WELL, I DON'T WANT TO LOOK AT ALL THAT JIGGLING FLESH. IT'S DISGUSTING.
THE JIGGLING WILL STOP WHEN I TURN THE CHAIR OFF.
I PULLED THE PLUG FIVE MINUTES AGO.
WHOA. TIME FOR A DIET.

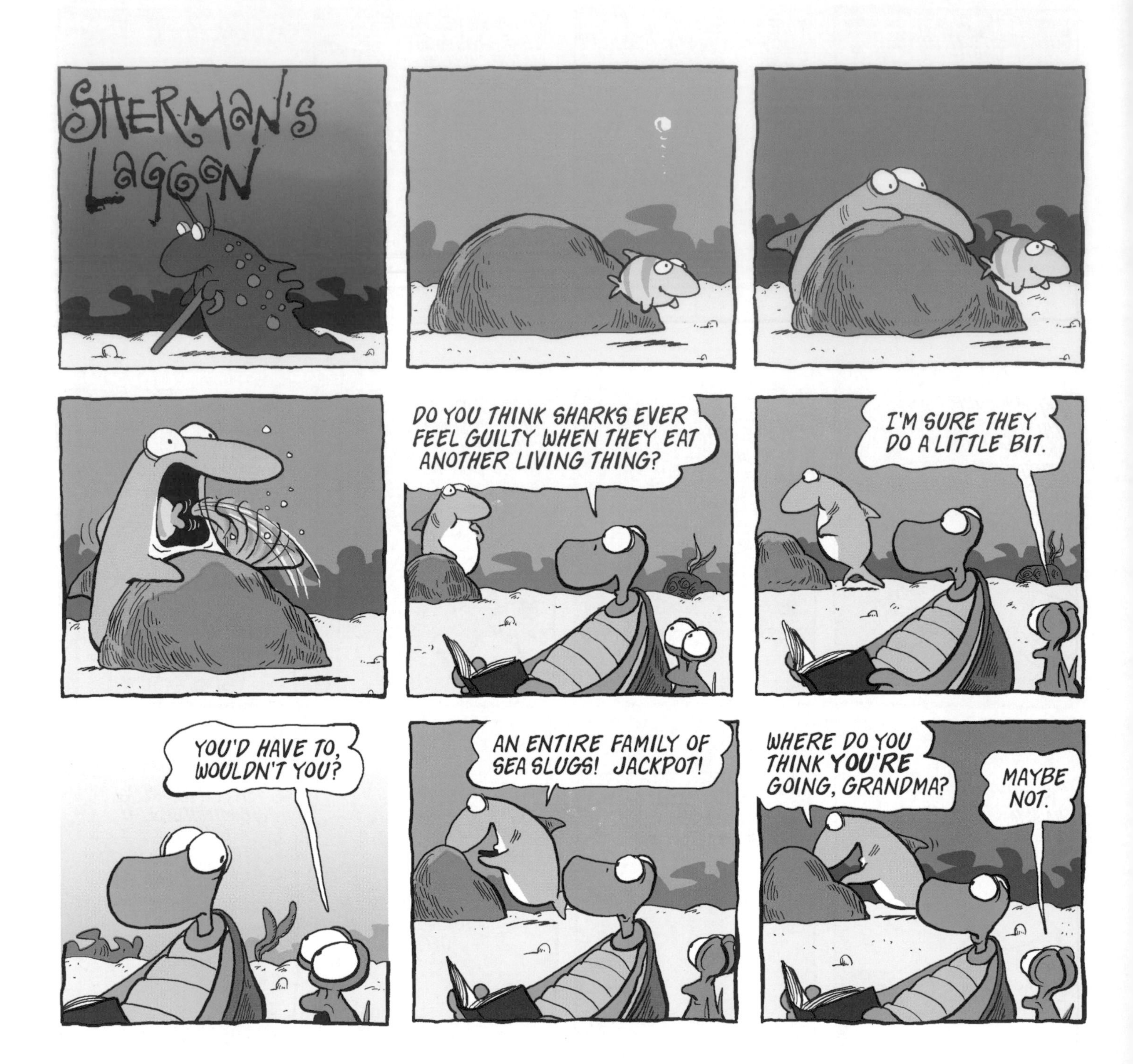
SHERMAN'S LAGOON
DO YOU THINK SHARKS EVER FEEL GUILTY WHEN THEY EAT ANOTHER LIVING THING?
I'M SURE THEY DO A LITTLE BIT.
YOU'D HAVE TO, WOULDN'T YOU?
AN ENTIRE FAMILY OF SEA SLUGS! JACKPOT!
WHERE DO YOU THINK **YOU'RE** GOING, GRANDMA?
MAYBE NOT.

LOOK AT THIS, SHERMAN. IT'S FROM THE YACHT WINE CELLAR.
OF COURSE, YOU WOULDN'T KNOW ABOUT THESE THINGS.
I'VE SEEN A BOTTLE OF THIS COGNAC ONLY ONCE BEFORE. IT'S QUITE RARE.
"WILD CHERRY BLAST"?
SUGAR-FREE.
HERE I AM LIVING IN THE LAP OF LUXURY AND STILL I'M NOT HAPPY. THERE'S SOMETHING MISSING IN MY LIFE.
I SHOULD BE DOING MORE THAN JUST SITTING AROUND ON SOME YACHT.
I'M AT THE PEAK OF MY LIFE, YOU KNOW... AT LEAST, I THINK I AM.
HOW LONG DO HERMIT CRABS LIVE, ANYWAY?
YOU'RE ASKING ME?

IS THAT A VIDEO OF HAWTHORNE MOLTING?
YEP. NOW IT'S ON THE INTERNET.
GROSS. I'VE NEVER SEEN A CRAB MOLT BEFORE.
APPARENTLY, IT'S A BIG HIT ON YOUTUBE.COM.
THAT'S AN OLD VIDEO.
HOW CAN YOU TELL?
IT'S FROM BEFORE HE REMOVED HIS "STYX RULES" TATOO.
THAT WAS A LONG AFTERNOON WITH A BRILLO PAD.

HAWTHORNE ARE YOU **SEWING**?
YEAH. I'VE DECIDED TO START A NEW BUSINESS.
YOU KNOW HOW BEACH APES ARE ALL ABOUT THEIR APPEARANCE?
AND THEY'LL BUY ANYTHING THAT MAKES THEM LOOK A LITTLE BETTER?
YEAH.
SO WHY ARE YOU MAKING THEM POT HOLDERS?
IT'S A HAIRPIECE!

HAWTHORNE, HOW DO EXPECT TO GO INTO BUSINESS MAKING HAIRPIECES FOR BEACH APES?
HUH?
Hawthorne's Hairpieces
WHAT DO YOU KNOW ABOUT HAIRSTYLES? YOU'VE GOT NO HAIR YOURSELF.
TRUE...
BUT I'VE GOT ACCESS TO SOMEONE WHO KNOWS HAIR!
WHAT'S THIS LOOK CALLED AGAIN?
THE "COWLICK." IT'S A CLASSIC.

HOW'S THE HAIRPIECE BUSINESS COMING, HAWTHORNE?
I CAN HARDLY KEEP UP.
Hawthorne's Hairpieces
BEACH APES ARE REQUESTING NEW STYLES, DIFFERENT COLORS.
Hawthorne's Hairpieces
DIFFERENT COLORS? HOW DO YOU DO DIFFERENT COLORS?
I'VE GOT A COLORIST. SHE'S GREAT.
Hawthorne's Hairpieces
SHOOT ME SOME AUBURN ON THIS ONE, CLAIRE.
VERY FUNNY. ONE BLACK COMING UP.

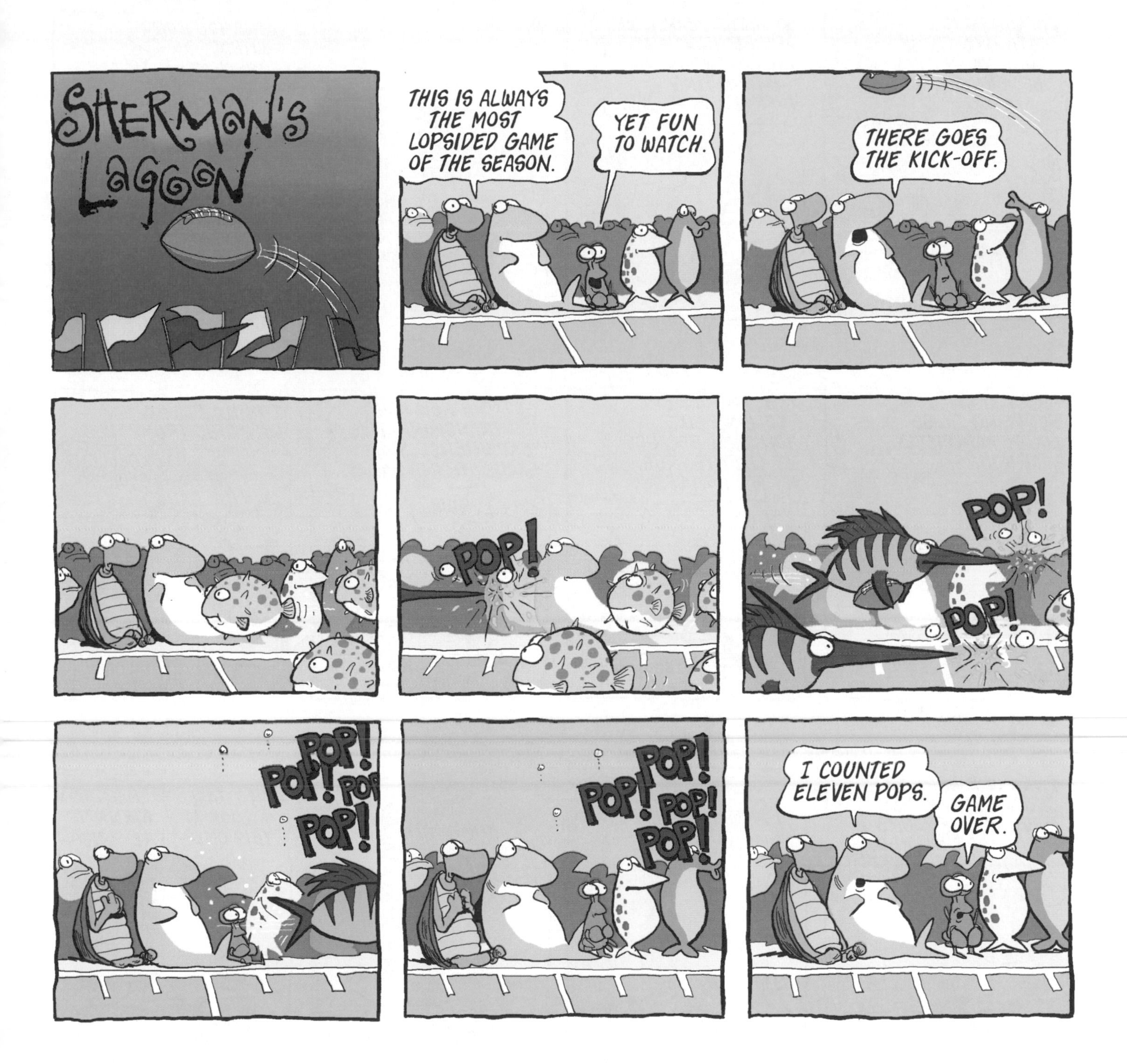
SHERMAN'S LAGOON
THIS IS ALWAYS THE MOST LOPSIDED GAME OF THE SEASON.
YET FUN TO WATCH.
THERE GOES THE KICK-OFF.
POP!
POP!
POP!
POP! POP! POP! POP!
POP! POP! POP! POP!
I COUNTED ELEVEN POPS.
GAME OVER.

DID YOU DO ANY TESTING ON THESE EXOTIC HAIRPIECES OF YOURS?
NO.
Hawthorne's Hairpieces
SO, THESE PEOPLE WHO ARE BUYING THEM, THEY MIGHT ACTUALLY BE PUTTING THEMSELVES AT RISK.
MMMM, POSSIBLY.
ANOTHER WEB ORDER. A CURLY BROWN. THEY'RE HOT.
WERE YOU BORN WITHOUT A CONSCIENCE?
HAD IT REMOVED. KEPT SLOWING ME DOWN.
ARE YOU STILL PEDDLING THOSE LOUSY HAIRPIECES OF YOURS?
HAWTHORNE'S HAIRPIECES
YES. AND THEY'RE SELLING LIKE HOTCAKES, BECAUSE MY CLIENTS TRUST MY FASHION SENSE.
GETTING NEW HAIR IS A TRANSFORMATIVE EXPERIENCE. YOU SHOULD TRY IT, BALDY.
HMPH.
I THINK I'LL GO WITH "THE TRUMP."
EXCELLENT CHOICE!
HAWTHORNE'S HAIRPIECES

I'VE COME HERE TO CHECK OUT THIS NEW BUSINESS OF YOURS. DO YOU CARRY WIGS, TOO?
HAVE WE GOT WIGS!
I'M INTRODUCING A WOMEN'S CELEBRITY LINE.
HMMMMMM...
HAWTHORNE' HAIRPIECES
CAN I TAKE A LOOK AT THIS ONE?
MARTHA STEWART PRE-PRISON.
HAWTHORNE'S HAIRPIECES

HAWTHORNE, I READ IN THE NEWSPAPER THAT YOUR WIGS CAUSE SCALP FUNGUS.
LIES! VICIOUS LIES!
HAWTHORNE'S HAIRPIECES
BUT, JUST TO BE ON THE SAFE SIDE, I'M CHANGING THE DIRECTION OF THE COMPANY.
REALLY? HOW SO?
HAWTHORNE'S HAIRPIECES
WELL, YOU KNOW WHAT THEY SAY... "WHEN LIFE GIVES YOU LEMONS, MAKE LEMONADE."
HAWTHORNE'S HAIRPIECES
SO, WHEN LIFE GIVES YOU FUNGUS?
MAKE BRIE.
Cheese by Hawthorne
HAWTHORNE, WHAT ON EARTH ARE YOU DOING?
UNG!
WELL, SINCE MY OCEAN ENERGY EXPERIMENT DIDN'T WORK, I'M TRYING SOMETHING DIFFERENT TO POWER THE LAGOON.
NUCULAR POWER!
DID HE SAY "NUCULAR"?
YOU'D PREFER COAL?
HAWTHORNE, THIS IS CRAZY! YOU CAN'T JUST PUT A NUCLEAR REACTOR IN YOUR CRAB HOLE.
WHY NOT?
BECAUSE YOU DON'T KNOW ABOUT THIS STUFF! IT COULD BE DANGEROUS!
IT'S ALL LAID OUT IN THIS HANDY KIT.
"LI'L HOME REACTOR"?
BOY, THAT SPONGEBOB WILL ENDORSE ANYTHING.

SHERMAN'S LAGOON
WHY ARE YOU TWO SITTING THERE DOING NOTHING WHILE THIS LAGOON GETS OVERRUN BY HAIRLESS BEACH APES?!
WHAT DO YOU EXPECT US TO DO?
YOU'RE SHARKS! EAT A FEW OF THEM, FOR CRYING OUT LOUD!
I'M NOT HUNGRY.
NEITHER AM I.
TWO FEROCIOUS GREAT WHITES, AND NEITHER ONE IS HUNGRY? ARE YOU KIDDIN' ME?
I KNOW YOU'VE GOT ROOM IN THERE. C'MON. WHADDYA SAY?
I'LL SPLIT ONE WITH YOU.
THAT'S THE SPIRIT.

HOW'S THAT SILLY "HOME" NUCLEAR POWER PLANT OF YOURS COMING ALONG, HAWTHORNE?
IT'S PRONOUNCED "NUCULAR"
THAT'S SCARY. YOU'RE TRYING TO OPERATE A NUCLEAR POWER PLANT AND YOU CAN'T EVEN PRONOUNCE THE WORD CORRECTLY.
I'M PRETTY SURE IT'S "NUCULAR."
YEP. IT'S "NUCULAR."
TWO AGAINST ONE. IT'S "NUCULAR."
BUT THE "TWO" ARE YOU GUYS!
I'M GOING OVER TO HAWTHORNE'S PLACE TO WATCH THE GAME.
ARE YOU NUTS?
HE'S GOT THAT STUPID HOME NUCLEAR POWER PLANT. WHO KNOWS WHAT COULD HAPPEN.
HAWTHORNE'S ASSURED ME THAT IT'S PERFECTLY SAFE TO BE AROUND.
HAVE YOU ALWAYS HAD THAT THIRD CLAW?
IT'S GREAT FOR WORKING THE SNACKS.
HAWTHORNE, WE INSIST THAT YOU REMOVE THIS NUCLEAR POWER PLANT FROM OUR LAGOON.
RELAX, BOYS, IT'S GONE. I SOLD THE WHOLE OPERATION.
YOU DID?
WHAT IF THAT TECHNOLOGY FALLS INTO THE WRONG HANDS?
WELL, THE WRONG PAWS, ACTUALLY.
WHOA! COOL!
MAYBE I SHOULD TRY "PUREE."

DID YOU NOTICE THAT THEY'RE BUILDING A PAINTBALL PARK NEAR HERE?
YES. AND I BET YOU'RE PRETTY JAZZED ABOUT IT.
WHY DOES EVERYONE THINK I'LL BE EXCITED ABOUT THIS?
BECAUSE YOU'RE BASICALLY A GIGANTIC KID.
AND YOU'RE HOLDING A PAINTBALL GUN.
SO I AM.

OUR FIRST PAINTBALL OUTING.
PAINTBALL PALACE IS JUST AN AWESOME PLACE.
I WONDER HOW LONG BEFORE WE GET INTO SOME REAL...
ZING!
WHOOSH!
SPLAT!
SPLAT!
ZIP!
SPLAT!
ZIP!
SPLAT!
SPLAT!
ACTION.
BOY. TOUGH RESTROOM.

ENEMY PAINTBALLS INCOMING, ERNEST! TAKE COVER! THEY'RE EVERYWHERE!
ZING!
SPLAT!
CAN YOU GET AN ESTIMATE OF THE FORCE WE'RE UP AGAINST? A PLATOON? MORE?
ZING!
ACTUALLY, JUST ONE.
WHO IS HE? RAMBO?
ZING!
SPLAT!
JIMBO.
YOU STINK AT THIS, WEENIE.

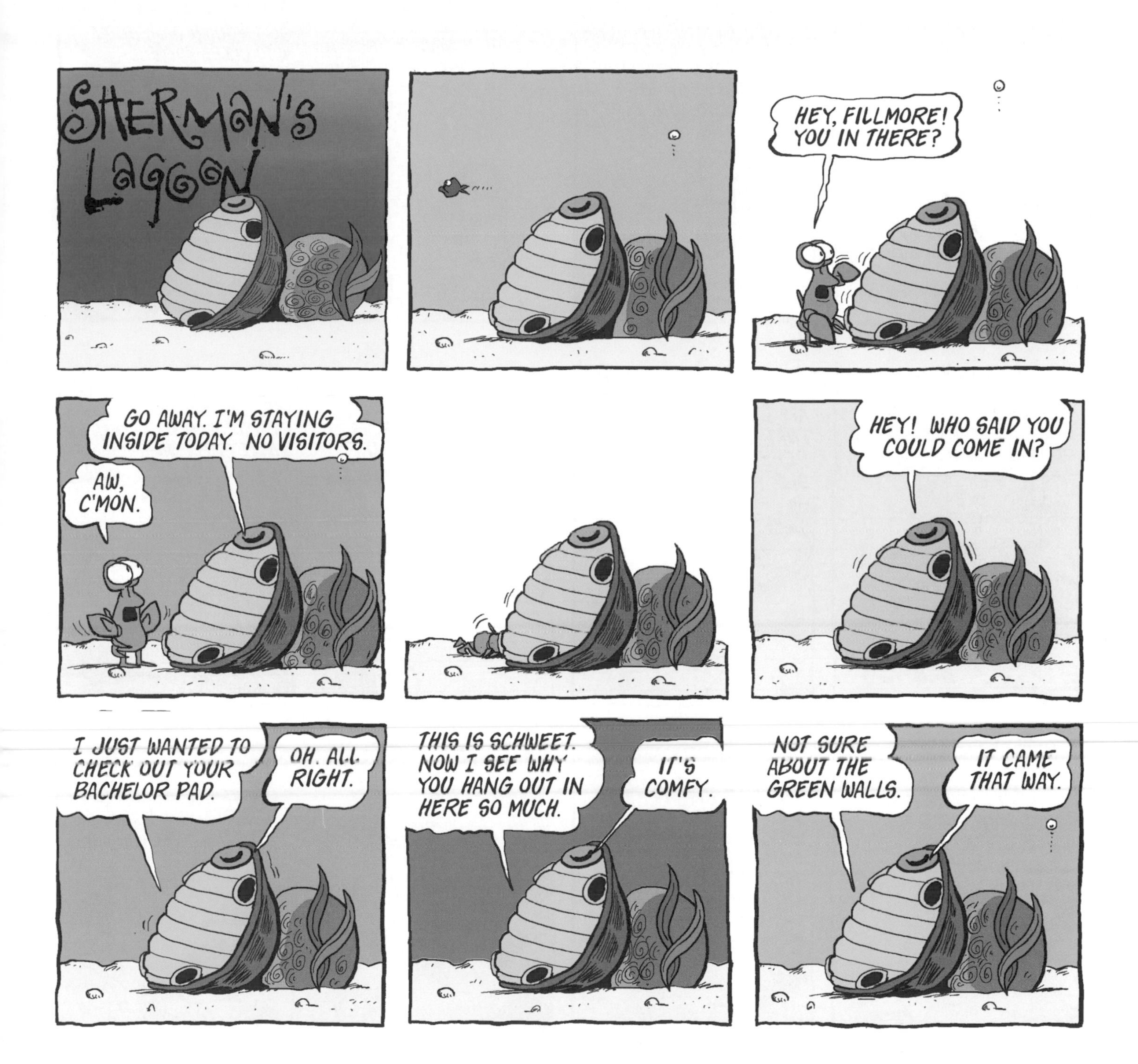
SHERMAN'S LAGOON
HEY, FILLMORE! YOU IN THERE?
GO AWAY. I'M STAYING INSIDE TODAY. NO VISITORS.
AW, C'MON.
HEY! WHO SAID YOU COULD COME IN?
I JUST WANTED TO CHECK OUT YOUR BACHELOR PAD.
OH. ALL RIGHT.
THIS IS SCHWEET. NOW I SEE WHY YOU HANG OUT IN HERE SO MUCH.
IT'S COMFY.
NOT SURE ABOUT THE GREEN WALLS.
IT CAME THAT WAY.

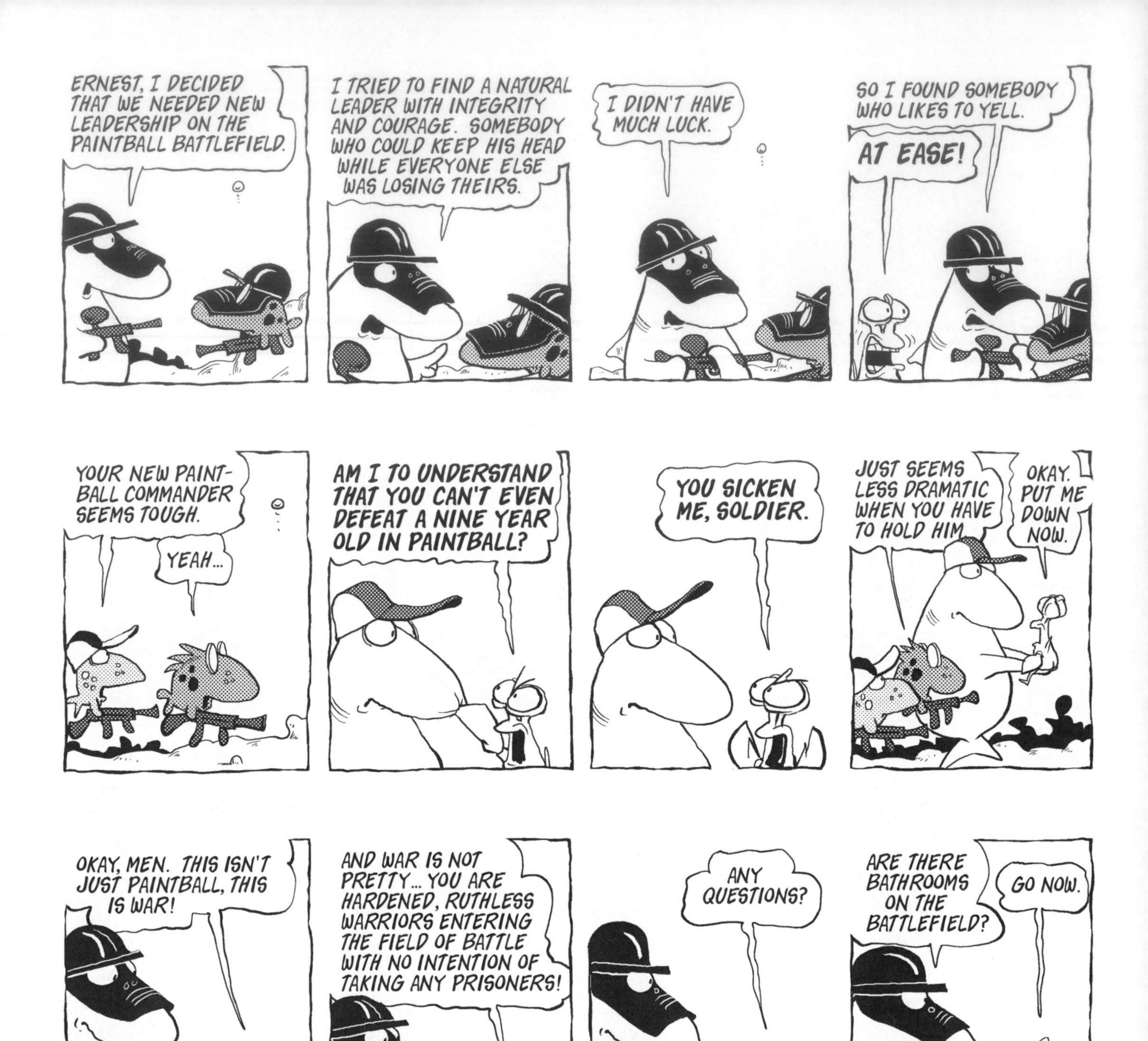
ERNEST, I DECIDED THAT WE NEEDED NEW LEADERSHIP ON THE PAINTBALL BATTLEFIELD.
I TRIED TO FIND A NATURAL LEADER WITH INTEGRITY AND COURAGE. SOMEBODY WHO COULD KEEP HIS HEAD WHILE EVERYONE ELSE WAS LOSING THEIRS.
I DIDN'T HAVE MUCH LUCK.
SO I FOUND SOMEBODY WHO LIKES TO YELL.
AT EASE!
YOUR NEW PAINT-BALL COMMANDER SEEMS TOUGH.
YEAH...
AM I TO UNDERSTAND THAT YOU CAN'T EVEN DEFEAT A NINE YEAR OLD IN PAINTBALL?
YOU SICKEN ME, SOLDIER.
JUST SEEMS LESS DRAMATIC WHEN YOU HAVE TO HOLD HIM.
OKAY. PUT ME DOWN NOW.
OKAY, MEN. THIS ISN'T JUST PAINTBALL, THIS IS WAR!
AND WAR IS NOT PRETTY... YOU ARE HARDENED, RUTHLESS WARRIORS ENTERING THE FIELD OF BATTLE WITH NO INTENTION OF TAKING ANY PRISONERS!
ANY QUESTIONS?
ARE THERE BATHROOMS ON THE BATTLEFIELD?
GO NOW.

MEN, WE'RE UP AGAINST A VERY DUG-IN ENEMY ON THE TOP OF THAT RIDGE.
ZING!
THIS IS GOING TO REQUIRE A DARING FRONTAL ASSAULT WITH A COORDINATED ATTACK FROM THE FLANK HERE.
ZING!
ANY QUESTIONS?
WHAT DO WE ONCE WE TAKE THE HILL?
CALL ME ON MY CELL PHONE.
YOU'RE NOT COMING?
ZING!
WHOA! THAT PAINTBALL ALMOST GOT ME!
THEY'VE GOT US PINNED DOWN.
ZING!
WHAT SHOULD WE DO?
HOLD OUR GROUND. HOPE THEY RUN OUT OF PAINTBALLS.
SPLAT!
SPLAT!
SOMEBODY MUST'VE CALLED IN AN AIRSTRIKE.
THAT WAS A SEA GULL.
WELL, THE PAINTBALL PARK IS CLOSED. WE LOST ALL OF OUR BATTLES TODAY.
LET'S FACE IT, ERNEST. I MAKE A LOUSY PAINTBALL WARRIOR. I'M A LOVER, NOT A FIGHTER.
BWAH HAHA HAHAHAHA!!
ISN'T YOUR WIFE MILES AWAY?
SHE HEARS EVERYTHING. IT'S CREEPY.

SHERMAN'S ON
SIT DOWN, MEGAN. YOU'RE IN FOR A TREAT TONIGHT.
FOR OUR FIRST COURSE, I'LL BE SERVING GOAT CHEESE EMPANADAS IN CURRY DOUGH, TOPPED WITH HOMEMADE RHUBARB SALSA...
...FOLLOWED BY CORONETS OF SALMON TARTARE...
...AND A SIDE OF BABY ASPARAGUS WITH A TANGERINE-OYSTER GLAZE...
FLAMBÉ!
POOF!
SO, WHADDAYA THINK OF THE NEW, GOURMET ME?
IS THAT A HAPPY CRY?
SNIFF

LOOKS LIKE WE'LL NEED A NEW MAYOR.
YEP. TOO BAD.
MAYOR JIM WAS A GOOD GUY. HE'LL BE HARD TO REPLACE. I LIKED HIS VISION.
SO WHY'D YOU EAT HIM?
HUNGER KNOWS NO POLITICS.
TOO BAD ABOUT MAYOR JIM. I GUESS I'LL TAKE THE JOB.
WHAT DO YOU MEAN?
I DO EVERYTHING ELSE AROUND HERE. MIGHT AS WELL BE MAYOR.
HMMM...
THE ELECTION'S JUST AROUND THE CORNER. MAYBE I'LL GIVE IT A SHOT.
YOU? YOU DON'T HAVE THE GUTS FOR POLITICS.
I'VE GOT A HUGE GUT.
WELL. THERE'S YOUR CAMPAIGN SLOGAN.

WELL, HAWTHORNE, I'M GOING TO RUN FOR MAYOR OF THE LAGOON. LOOKS LIKE IT'S YOU AND ME, MANO-A-MANO.
I'M OFFICIALLY THROWING MY HAT IN THE RING.
I TRUST YOUR NEWSPAPER WILL HAVE FAIR AND BALANCED COVERAGE.
PAPER ENDORSES HAWTHORNE FOR MAYOR.
TURTLE THROWS HAT, INJURES SENIOR... STORY PAGE 4.

I SUPPOSE YOU'VE HEARD BY NOW THAT I'M RUNNING FOR MAYOR OF THE LAGOON.
NO, I HAVEN'T

OH WELL... GOOD. THIS'LL GIVE ME A CHANCE TO PERSONALLY ANSWER ANY QUESTIONS YOU MIGHT HAVE.

WHY DO YOU SOUND LIKE A GIRL ON THE PHONE?
POLITICAL QUESTIONS.

HELLO, GOOD CITIZENS OF KAPUPU LAGOON. CAN I COUNT ON YOUR VOTE FOR MAYOR?
WHY DO YOU WANT TO BE MAYOR?

BECAUSE OF THE ABSOLUTE POWER OVER EVERYONE'S LIVES!

BWAHHHH HA HA HA HA HA HA HA HA HA!

HE LOST ME WITH THE EVIL LAUGH.
THAT'S HOW HE ALWAYS LAUGHS.

I SEE FILLMORE HAS LEFT SOME OF HIS CAMPAIGN LITERATURE WITH YOU.
YEP. HE WAS JUST HERE.
DON'T BELIEVE A WORD HE SAYS. THESE POLITICAL WANNA-BE'S WILL SAY ANYTHING TO GET ELECTED.
WHAT DID HE SAY?
HE SAID YOU, TOO, WOULD MAKE A FINE MAYOR.
HOGWASH!

SHERMAN'S LAGOON
WHADDYA THINK OF THIS BRACELET WITH THE BLUE DRESS?
IT WORKS.
YOU GUYS GOING OUT TONIGHT?
YEP.
SPORTS WEEK
IS THE SCARF OVERKILL?
I SAY GO FOR IT.
AND SHE USES YOU AS A FASHION CONSULTANT?
IT'S A COUPLE THING.
TOO MUCH MASCARA?
LOOKS GREAT.
THE HUSBAND IS THE FIRST LINE OF DEFENSE AGAINST FASHION BLUNDERS.
EVERY NOW AND THEN SHE'LL THROW SOMETHING IN TO SEE IF I'M PAYING ATTENTION. GOTTA WATCH OUT FOR THAT.
HOW ABOUT THE ELEPHANT EARS?
LOVE IT.

IF ELECTED MAYOR, WHAT WILL YOU DO ABOUT OUR SCHOOLS?
ELECTION 200
I'LL FORM A COMMITTEE THAT WILL STUDY THE EFFECTIVENESS OF THE CURRENT COMMITTEE.
I WON'T DO NOTHING. KIDS NEED TO LEARN THEMSELVES. IT'S TOUGH OUT THERE.
WE'RE MOVING.
OKAY. LET'S GO SIT BY THE CONCESSION STAND.

WE'RE CONDUCTING AN EXIT POLL. COULD YOU TELL US WHICH CANDIDATE YOU VOTED FOR?
VOTE HER
NEITHER ONE. YOU'RE A NINCOMPOOP WHO COULDN'T RUN A KINDERGARTEN, AND YOU'RE A SLIMEBALL WHO CAN'T BE TRUSTED.
VOTE HAWTHORN
I'M JUST THANKFUL THIS WHOLE UGLY THING IS OVERWITH.
LOOKS LIKE ALL THAT NEGATIVE MESSAGING PAID OFF.
FOR BOTH OF US.

THE ELECTION RESULTS ARE IN, AND NEITHER ONE OF YOU WON.
HUH? THERE WAS NOBODY ELSE RUNNING!
THERE WAS A HEAVY TURNOUT FOR A CERTAIN WRITE-IN CANDIDATE.
WHO?
"NONE OF THE ABOVE."
HUMILIATING.
BEATEN BY A NUN.

LET'S SEE, LET'S SEE... SO MANY CHOICES...
OH, COME ON, FILLMORE!
JUST STEP AND ORDER YOUR COFFEE LIKE A MAN!
I'LL HAVE A VENTI, HALF-CAF, PEPPERMINT, NON-FAT MOCHA WITH WHIPPED CREAM AND A CHERRY ON TOP, PLEASE.
AND JUST HOW IS THAT MANLY?
NO SLEEVE, BABY!
NOBODY AROUND HERE GETS ME.
WELL...
MAYBE THAT'S BECAUSE YOU'RE ALWAYS ACTING LIKE A MACHO JERK...
YOU CONSTANTLY PUT EVERYONE DOWN, AND YOU'D TAKE THE LUNCH MONEY FROM A CHILD IF YOU HAD HALF A CHANCE.
JUST A THOUGHT.
CAN WE GO BACK TO THE INK STAIN THINGIES?

FILLMORE, YOU ACT LIKE A SMART GUY. I WANT TO START ANOTHER BUSINESS. WHAT INDUSTRIES ARE HOT?
WELL, YOU CAN'T GO WRONG IF IT INVOLVES THE ENVIRONMENT.
YOU MEAN IN A POSITIVE WAY?
PREFERABLY.

SHERMAN'S LAGOON
WHAT ARE YOU ALL BUMMED ABOUT, FAT BOY?
I FEEL LIKE LIFE IS PASSING ME BY, HAWTHORNE.
I WAKE UP, SWIM AROUND, EAT A FISH, GO TO BED... WHAT'S IT ALL ABOUT?
GOT ME.
WHEN IT'S ALL OVER, WILL I HAVE REALLY DONE ANYTHING?
SURE.
WILL ANYBODY REALLY MISS ME?
YOUR FRIENDS WILL MISS YOU.
THAT'S WHAT GIVES LIFE ITS MEANING, SHERMAN...
... THE FRIENDS YOU MAKE ALONG THE WAY.
WHO?
I DUNNO! SOMEBODY MUST BE YOUR FRIEND!

SO WHAT KIND OF BUSINESS WOULD HELP THE ENVIRONMENT?
WELL...
HOW ABOUT A RECYCLING FACILITY? THE LAGOON COULD REALLY USE ONE.
YEAH.
THAT PROBABLY WOULD BE MORE EARTH FRIENDLY THAN MY CURRENT PROJECT.
WHICH IS?
A LINE OF STYROFOAM CLOTHES.
THEY'RE SQUEAKY.
THANK YOU ALL FOR COMING TO MY GRAND OPENING.
Hawthorne's Recycling
I HOPE THIS WILL SERVE THE LAGOON IN A POSITIVE WAY FOR YEARS TO COME.
AND NOW, IN A SYMBOLIC GESTURE, I'D LIKE TO THROW OUT THE FIRST RECYCLABLE.
I'D HAVE PREFERRED A SIMPLE RIBBON CUTTING.
TA-DAH!
Hawthorne's Recycling

HAWTHORNE, I'D LIKE TO BE YOUR FIRST RECYCLING CUSTOMER.
WHAT'S THIS?
Hawthorne's Recycling
IT'S ALL THE STUFF THAT CAN BE RECYCLED.
SO GO PUT IT IN THE PROPER BINS!
I THOUGHT YOU INVENTED SOME AUTOMATIC PROCESS THAT DID THAT!
THAT WAS JUST A BUNCH OF P.R. ... I'M NOT TOUCHING SOMEBODY ELSE'S GARBAGE!
ME? VICE PRESIDENT OF SORTING CONSULTATION?
THE JOB'S YOURS IF YOU WANT IT.

SO, WHAT'S MY JOB AT THE RECYCLING CENTER?
WELL, WHEN FOLKS BRING IN THEIR TRASH...
YOU PULL OUT THE RECYCLABLES AND PUT THEM INTO THE PROPER BINS... PAPER, GLASS, ETC.
Hawthorne's Recycling
SO BASICALLY, I'M ROOTING THROUGH GARBAGE ALL DAY.
UM, YEAH.
CAN I BRING A FORK?
FINE. BUT YOU DON'T GET A LUNCH BREAK.
OKAY, HAWTHORNE, I HAVE A BUNCH OF RECYCLABLES FOR YOU. WHERE'S THE PAPER GO?
IN THAT BIN OVER THERE.
HOW ABOUT THE ALUMINUM?
RIGHT HERE.
Hawthorne's Recycling
GLASS?
OVER HERE.
A.O.L. TRIAL DISKS?
IN HERE.
HERE, SHERMAN, WHY DON'T YOU TAKE ALL THIS SCRAP PAPER TO THE RECYCLING CENTER.
HEY, WHAT'S THIS?
... AMAZON BOOKS ORDER CONFIRMATION.
"CONTROLLING YOUR HUSBAND THROUGH HYPNOSIS"?
ON THREE, YOU WILL THINK YOU'RE A CHICKEN.

SHERMAN'S LAGOON
YOU'RE NEW. WHAT BRINGS YOU TO THESE PARTS?
I'M TAKING A LITTLE ISLAND VACATION.
THANKSGIVING IS OVER, AND I MADE IT... JUST BARELY.
YEAH, I SEE. BETTER PUT ON SOME SUN BLOCK.
THANKS.
IT'S A SPECIAL ISLAND FORMULA MADE WITH COCONUT AND PAPAYA.
SMELLS GOOD.
HUNGRY?
STARVED.
TRY THESE TROPICAL BREAD STICKS. THEY'RE AWESOME.
THANKS. YOU'RE A NICE LITTLE CRAB.
WELCOME TO OUR ISLAND. IF YOU NEED ANYTHING ELSE, JUST HOLLER.
WILL DO.
HE'S BASTED AND STUFFED.
NOW WE WAIT.

BOX OF STUFF FROM THORNTON.
THORNTON? WHAT COULD HE POSSIBLY HAVE TO RECYCLE?
Hawthorne's Recycling
LOOKS LIKE JUST BOOKS. ALL HIS OLD TOM CLANCY NOVELS. HE ALWAYS SEEMED TO BE READING ONE.
INTERESTING.
Hawthorne'
THE OLD NANCY DREW MYSTERIES INSIDE THE TOM CLANCY COVER TRICK, EH?
WILL A SMOOTHIE HUSH THIS UP?
YOU CLOSED THE RECYCLING CENTER? WHY?
PROFIT MARGINS JUST WEREN'T THERE.
CLOSED
Hawthorne's Recycling
NOT EVERYTHING'S ABOUT PROFIT! WHAT ABOUT THE GOOD YOU WERE DOING FOR THE ENVIRONMENT?
THE ENVIRONMENT? WHAT'S THE STUPID ENVIRONMENT EVER DONE FOR ME?
GIVEN YOU A HOME!
YEAH, A HOME FULL OF WHINERS. THANKS, ENVIRONMENT.

WHAT THE HECK IS THIS NEW SCAM?
INSTANT COMPANIONSHIP.
PET SHELLS $4.95
BUT THIS IS JUST AN EMPTY SHELL.
NOT UNLIKE YOUR LOVE LIFE.
SO YOU THINK INSULTING ME WILL MAKE A SALE?
YOU WANT A FRIEND OR NOT?
GIVE ME THE SPECKLED ONE.

IS THAT ONE OF HAWTHORNE'S PET SHELLS?
YEAH. FUNNY, HUH?
I'M THINKING ABOUT GETTING ONE, BUT A PET IS SUCH A COMMITMENT.
YOU ALWAYS HAVE TO KEEP AN EYE ON THEM.
SPEAKING OF KEEPING AN EYE ON THINGS...
THERE GOES YOUR CHILD.
SEE? JUST THINK IF THAT WERE A PET.
MEGAN, LOOK. I BOUGHT ONE OF HAWTHORNE'S PET SHELLS.
THAT'S KIND OF CUTE.
PET SHELL
COSMO
I ALSO BOUGHT THE OWNER'S GUIDE AND EXTENDED WARRANTY.
UH, HUH.
PET SHELL
AND AN ENTIRE WARDROBE. CLOTHES FOR EVERY OCCASION.
YEAH.
PET SHELL
ALL CUTENESS IS GONE AT THIS POINT.
TRAINING BISCUITS, UH...
PET SHELL

SHERMAN, HOW ON EARTH DID YOU FALL FOR THIS "PET SHELL" SCAM?
IT'S JUST AN OLD SHELL WITH SOME IMAGINATIVE PACKAGING.
BUT IT MAKES ME HAPPY. I LIKE CARING FOR THINGS, EVEN IF THEY'RE IMAGINARY PETS.
YOUR SON JUST HEAVED HIS COOKIES.
YOUR TURN, MEGAN.

SHERMAN'S LAGOON
THROW AWAY THAT BULKY iPOD, HAWTHORNE, AND GET YOURSELF AN iCHIP.
A WHAT?
IT'S A CHIP THAT GETS SURGICALLY IMPLANTED IN YOUR BRAIN.
IT STORES 20 MILLION SONGS.
NO KIDDIN'.
ALL I HAVE TO DO IS THINK OF A SONG AND IT JUST PLAYS IN MY HEAD.
ANY SONG? LIKE, FOR INSTANCE, "I'M A LITTLE TEAPOT"?
IT JUST STARTED PLAYING.
HOW ABOUT "THE MACARENA"?
OOH... NOT "THE MACARENA."
YOU KNOW, FAT BOY, YOU SHOULD LEARN TO RECOGNIZE WHEN TECHNOLOGY HAS GONE TOO FAR.
LET'S HEAR "I'M A LITTLE TEAPOT" AGAIN.
STOP!

"THE PET SHELL CARE MANUAL"? YOU **BOUGHT** ONE OF THOSE STUPID PET SHELL THINGS?
LOWER YOUR VOICE. HE'S RIGHT HERE.
SHERMAN, REMEMBER THE "PET ROCK"? SAME THING. IT'S JUST A GIMMICK.
DID YOU KNOW PET SHELLS NEED TO BATHE TWICE A DAY?
The Pet Shell Care Manual
HELLO? ARE YOU SERIOUS?
"BE SURE TO KEEP YOUR PET SHELL IN A WARM PLACE AT NIGHT."
The Pet Shell Care Manual
"THE PET SHELL IS ILLEGAL IN TWELVE STATES."
THERE YOU GO.
The Pet Shell Care Manual
HAWTHORNE, I THINK MY PET SHELL IS DEAD.
SHERMAN, I DON'T THINK YOU REALLY GET IT, DO YOU?
PET SHELLS $4.95
YOUR "PET SHELL" WAS NEVER ALIVE. IT'S JUST A GIMMICK... ANOTHER ONE OF MY SCAMS. I'M ALMOST SORRY I TOOK YOUR MONEY.
SO, THERE'S NOTHING YOU CAN DO?
NO.
PET SHELLS $4.95
DO YOU SELL LITTLE CASKETS?
OUR CARDBOARD MODEL.... TEN BUCKS.
PET SHELLS $4.95

SO, WE FIND OURSELVES ON THE PAINTBALL BATTLEFIELD ONCE AGAIN IN DIRE STRAIGHTS.
THE ENEMY IS ALL AROUND US. WE'LL HAVE TO MAKE SURE WE DON'T LEAVE OURSELVES OPEN.
FWAP!
FWAP!
FWAP!
FWAP!
FWAP!
FWAP!
I LEFT MY REAR FLANK EXPOSED.
TO BE FAIR, IT'S AN AWFUL LOT OF FLANK.

Lagoon Paintball Park
Lagoon Paintball Park
UM, "THE GOOD, THE BAD, AND THE UGLY"?
THOSE WERE HAND SIGNALS, NOT CHARADES.

THERE'S OUR PAINTBALL NEMESIS, JIMBO. HE'S TOUGH.
WE'VE TRIED EVERYTHING. HE HAS NO WEAKNESSES.
JIMMY!
YOU GET HOME RIGHT THIS INSTANT!
WELL, MAYBE ONE.
DINNERTIME.
FIRE!

YOU REALIZE HERMAN'S FOURTH BIRTHDAY IS COMING UP AND WE HAVE NOTHING PLANNED.
PHONE BOOK
WHAT DID YOU HAVE IN MIND?
WELL, WE COULD GET A PONY AND HAVE A PARTY AND GIVE PONY RIDES.
PHONE BOOK
WE'RE SHARKS, MEGAN. SHARKS CAN'T RIDE PONIES.
YOU THINK OF SOMETHING.
PHONE BOOK
CAN WE EAT THE PONY?
NO!
PHONE BOOK

SHERMAN'S LAGOON
BOY, LOOK AT ALL THE PEOPLE ON THE PIER TODAY.
LOOKS LIKE A BUS LOAD OF TOURISTS JUST ARRIVED.
I THINK THEY SEE US.
SMILE FOR THE VIDEO CAMERAS.
LOOKS LIKE YOUR WIFE IS GOING TO MAKE THE EVENING NEWS AGAIN.
WHO'D SHE EAT THIS TIME?

THE FIRST THING WE NEED TO DO IN PLANNING HERMAN'S BIRTHDAY PARTY IS TO ESTABLISH A BUDGET.
GOOD IDEA.
LET'S SEE... WE'LL NEED A CAKE AND INVITATIONS... A CLOWN WOULD BE NICE...
HOW MUCH IS THAT BASEBALL CARD OF YOURS WORTH?
IS THAT A RELATED TOPIC?
I HEARD MEGAN'S THROWING QUITE THE BIRTHDAY BASH FOR HERMAN.
IT'S GETTING OUT OF CONTROL.
YOU SHOULD SEE THE CAKE SHE'S MAKING. IT'S RIGHT OUT OF MARTHA STEWART'S MAGAZINE.
THAT CARROT CAKE IN THE NOVEMBER ISSUE?
YOU READ MARTHA?
EVERY NOW AND THEN SHE THROWS IN LITTLE TIPS ON HOW TO SURVIVE IN PRISON.
I FIGURE AT SOME POINT I'LL BE GOING.
YOU **ARE** OVERDUE.
HOW COME I HAVEN'T BEEN INVITED TO HERMAN'S BIRTHDAY PARTY?
ERNEST, HE'S TURNING FOUR!
YEAH, BUT I HEARD MEGAN'S BOOKED ALL KINDS OF COOL ACTS.
SHE HAS? LIKE WHAT?
DID THE BLUE ANGELS JUST SPELL "HAPPY BIRTHDAY HERMAN"?
MEGAN!

NOTHING'S GOING RIGHT FOR HERMAN'S PARTY!
IT'S OKAY.
HAPPY BIR
IT'S NOT OKAY! DAVID COPPERFIELD CANCELLED AND BLUE MAN GROUP GOT LOST FINDING THE PLACE!
WHAT ELSE CAN POSSIBLY RUIN THIS PARTY?
BIRT
HEY, GUYS, PARIS HILTON JUST SHOWED UP.
SECURITY!

WELL, MEGAN, I MUST SAY, YOU'VE PUT ON A VERY TASTEFUL BIRTHDAY PARTY FOR YOUR CHILD. MARTHA STEWART WOULD BE PROUD.
THANK YOU.

MATCHING "DORA THE EXPLORER" NAPKINS AND CAKE.... THE SPONGEBOB CENTERPIECE... YOU'VE THOUGHT OF EVERYTHING.

AND THE PIÑATA IS A NICE TOUCH.

WE DIDN'T GET A PINATA.
TAKE HIM DOWN!

FILLMORE, HAVE YOU SEEN MY HUSBAND?
YEAH.
HE'S A BIG, GRAY, CHILDISH SHARK. RIGHT?
DOESN'T YOUR HEAD USUALLY COME OUT THE OTHER HOLE?
DON'T JOKE WITH MEGAN TODAY.

SHERMAN'S

GUESS WHAT I GOT AT SAM'S CLUB.
SOMETHING LARGE, I'M SURE.

CHECK THIS OUT.
PUMP PUMP PUMP

TA DAH! FROSTY THE SNOWMAN!

WAIT. THAT'S NOT ALL.

PUMP PUMP PUMP PUMP

TA DAH! HOMER SIMPSON SANTA!

NOTHING SAYS "MERRY CHRISTMAS" LIKE ENORMOUS, INFLATABLE LAWN ORNAMENTS.

HOMER OR FROSTY?
I'LL TAKE FROSTY.

I SEE YOU GOT YOURSELF A LANCE ARMSTRONG BRACELET.
WELL...
NOT EXACTLY.
WHAT IS IT?
I WANTED A MORE SHARK-SPECIFIC MESSAGE THAN "LIVE STRONG."
CHECK IT OUT.
"EAT OFTEN"?
WEARING ONE OF THOSE RUBBER BRACELETS, I SEE.
YEP.
IT'S NOT JUST TRENDY, IT'S FOR A GREAT CAUSE.
YOU SHOULD GET YOURSELF ONE.
I DON'T THINK I COULD WEAR A RUBBER BAND AROUND MY CLAW.
IT'S A LITTLE TOO "LOBSTER TANK."
OH, RIGHT.

THOUGHT YOU DIDN'T LIKE THE RUBBER BRACELET TREND.
YEAH, BUT I FOUND ONE THAT CAPTURES MY PERSPECTIVE ON LIFE PERFECTLY.
SO, IT'S NOT A "LIVE STRONG" BRACELET?
NO.
"LIVE WITH A CHIP ON YOUR SHOULDER"?
YOU GOT A PROBLEM WITH THAT?

LOOKS LIKE BOB THE BOTTOM DWELLER GOT HIMSELF A RUBBER BRACELET.
DOES IT SAY "LIVE STRONG" LIKE MINE?
LET'S SEE...
CLOSE.
"SMELL STRONG"
BURP!

HEY, WALTER, DID YOU GET ONE OF THOSE "LIVE STRONG" BRACELETS TOO?
NOT EXACTLY.
MINE SAYS "LIVE IN FEAR."
THAT'S NOT VERY POSITIVE.
WHAM!
PRACTICAL, THOUGH.
UNGH.

GOT YOURSELF ONE OF THOSE RUBBER "LIVE STRONG" BRACELETS, HUH?
MINE SAYS "LIVE NATURAL."
IT REPRESENTS MY NEW PHILOSOPHY.
WHICH IS?
DON'T BUY INTO SOCIETY'S RULES ON HYGIENE.
WHAT SMELLS LIKE A LOCKER ROOM?
WILD KINGDOM OVER HERE.

SHERMAN'S LAGOON
HORS D'OEUVRE?
AUGH!
THERE GOES THE CATERER.
SAW THAT COMING.
HEY! WHERE DO YOU THINK YOU'RE GOING? GET BACK OVER TO THE SHRIMP BOWL!
GO ON!
ELECTRIC EEL COMING THROUGH! BACK OFF!
BRRZZZZT!
THESE LAGOON HOLIDAY PARTIES ALWAYS GET A LITTLE WEIRD.
AVOID THE MISTLETOE.

WHAT ARE YOU WATCHING?
HAWTHORNE'S TOE PINCHING CONCERT.
HE CAN ACTUALLY GET A MELODY GOING WITH THEIR SCREAMS.
WHAT'S THE HOLD UP?
I NEED A TENOR TOE.
WHAT'S IT LIKE TO FLY, DREW?
OH MY, IT'S UNBELIEVABLE.
IT'S THE MOST EXHILERATING, LIFE-AFFIRMING FEELING YOU CAN IMAGINE, HAVING THE WIND IN YOUR WINGS, GAZING AT THE LAND-LOCKED WORLD BELOW.
WHAT'S IT LIKE TO SWIM?
WET.
YOU REALLY CAN PAINT THE PICTURE.

SHERMAN, ARE YOU TELLING ME THAT AFTER ALL THESE YEARS AS A SHARK, YOU'RE JUST NOW FEELING GUILTY ABOUT ALL THE THINGS YOU'VE EATEN?
UH HUH. ALL THOSE FISH, ALL THOSE BEACH APES, THE PONIES AND THE POODLES...
...THE LIVES I'VE RUINED.
WHAT ABOUT MY LIFE?
THAT'S DIFFERENT. WE'RE MARRIED.

MEGAN TELLS ME YOU'RE BEGINNING TO FEEL GUILTY ABOUT ALL THE THINGS YOU'VE EATEN.
I AM.
DON'T YOU EVER FEEL GUILTY ABOUT ALL THE TOES YOU'VE PINCHED?
HECK NO!
I EVEN LEAVE ONE OF THESE BEHIND...
"YOU'VE BEEN PINCHED BY HAWTHORNE..."
"... AVAILABLE FOR WEDDINGS, PARTIES AND BAR MITZVAHS."
REASONABLE RATES.
STILL FEELING REMORSE OVER ALL THE THINGS YOU'VE EATEN?
SIGH
I CAN'T GET PAST IT.
IT'S NOT YOUR FAULT. IT'S NATURE.
YOU'RE A MINDLESS, THOUGHTLESS, BIG, DUMB EATING MACHINE.
EVEN YOUR KIND WORDS DON'T COMFORT ME.
I'VE GOT MORE.
STILL FEELING GUILTY ABOUT ALL THE STUFF YOU'VE EATEN, SHERMAN?
I CAN'T SHAKE IT.
WHAT IF YOU COULD MAKE CONTACT WITH THEM AND TELL THEM YOU'RE SORRY?
HOW?
MADAME TURBOT. SHE CAN REACH THE OTHER SIDE.
REALLY?
IS THIS COSTLY?
THE ROAMING CHARGES CAN GET A LITTLE PRICEY.

SHERMAN'S LAGOON
HONK!
HEY, FILLMORE, WHAT ARE YOU UP TO TONIGHT?
NOTHING. GO AWAY.
OH, C'MON! IT'S NEW YEAR'S EVE!
IT'S JUST ANOTHER DAY.
BUT WHEN THE CLOCK STRIKES TWELVE, IT'LL BE A NEW YEAR!
AND I'LL BE IN BED.
LOSER!
NEW YEAR'S EVE IS JUST A BUNCH OF FORCED REVELRY.
I DO NOT REACT WELL TO SITUATIONS WHERE I'M FORCED TO REVEL.
AW C'MON! IT'S ALMOST MIDNIGHT! LET'S MAKE SOME NOISE! WHOO HOO!
SHOULD AULD ACQUAINTANCE BE FORGOT...
REVEL!
NO!

WE'VE REACHED THE OTHER SIDE, AND ONE OF YOUR PAST VICTIMS WOULD LIKE TO SPEAK WITH YOU.
UNCLE BOB? I ATE YOU?
AT THE NEW YEARS EVE PARTY TWO YEARS AGO!
THAT WAS YOU? I THOUGHT YOU WERE THE SALMON PLATTER!
MY LAST WORDS WERE...
"DON'T EAT ME! I'M NOT THE SALMON PLATTER!"
COME ON, THAT'S PRETTY VAGUE.
ANOTHER ONE OF YOUR VICTIMS IS WITH US.
WHO ARE YOU?
BABE RUTH. YOU ATE ME!
NO I DIDN'T! YOU DIED BEFORE I WAS BORN!
I JUST ALWAYS WANTED TO BE IN A COMIC STRIP.
BAD BAMBINO!
ONE LAST VICTIM OF YOURS WANTS TO MAKE CONTACT FROM THE OTHER SIDE.
BRING IT ON.
POOF!
HEY, YOU LOOK VAGUELY FAMILIAR.
I SHOULD! YOU ATE ME FOR BREAKFAST THIS MORNING!
I DID, HUH?
SO, HOW'D THE REST OF YOUR DAY GO?
PEACHY.